HEBREW SYNTAX: An Outline

HEBREW SYNTAX
An Outline

second edition

Ronald J. Williams

University of Toronto Press

Toronto Buffalo London

First edition
©University of Toronto Press 1967
Reprinted 1970, 1974

Second edition
©University of Toronto Press 1976
Toronto   Buffalo   London
Reprinted 1978, 1980, 1982, 1984

Printed in Canada

ISBN 0-8020-2218-9
LC 75-44271

Canadian Cataloguing in Publication Data

Williams, Ronald J., 1917-
  Hebrew syntax

  Includes indexes.
  Bibliography: p.
  ISBN 0-8020-2218-9

  1. Hebrew language - Syntax.   I. Title.

  PJ4701. W55 1976   492.4'5   C76-003025-1

To

THEOPHILE JAMES MEEK

(1881–1966)

אַשְׁרֵי אָדָם מָצָא חָכְמָה
וְאָדָם יָפִיק תְּבוּנָה

(Pr 3:13)

Preface to First Edition

In offering this modest contribution to Hebrew studies,
I am acutely aware of my indebtedness to a host of scho-
lars. The brief bibliography at the end of this book is
but a partial indication of this debt. To all, especially those who graciously read the manuscript in its earlier stages, I would express my obligation and gratitude.

The greatest debt of all, however, I owe to the late
Professor T. J. Meek whose memory I revere as teacher,
colleague and friend. His profound understanding of the
principles of Hebrew syntax was the stimulation which
aroused my special interest in the subject, and which
resulted in this volume.

For many years he taught a course in Hebrew syntax
which greatly enhanced Hebrew studies in the University
of Toronto. When this duty passed to me on his retirement, it was his inspiration and never-failing help that
afforded me courage to assume the task. We had hoped
that during his retirement he would provide us with the
long-awaited fruits of his lifetime studies. Ill health,
alas, prevented this, and the present work must serve as
a poor substitute. That I have dedicated it to him is a
small token of my esteem and gratitude.

From the many students who have attended my classes
all through the years I have learned much. As one of the
sages observed long ago: הרבה למדתי מרבותי ומחברי יותר
מרבותי ומתלמידי יותר מכלם. To them all I offer my heart-
felt thanks.

R. J. Williams
University of Toronto
April 20, 1967

vii

Preface to Second Edition

The wide use being made of this manual has encouraged me to take the opportunity of a fourth printing to revise and slightly expand the text. In response to the request of a number of users, all the Hebrew examples which are quoted have been provided with translations. It is hoped that this will assist in clarifying the syntactic features which they illustrate.

Both in the bibliography and the text some account has been taken of recent studies. Outstanding among these is the work of Professor F. I. Andersen, whose thorough analysis of non-verbal clauses in the Pentateuch is a model of what such a study should be.

The lack of a subject index in the first edition led Professor Douglas Knight of Vanderbilt University, assisted by four of his graduate students, to prepare one for their own use. For their kind permission to incorporate this valuable compilation into the new edition of this volume I am most grateful.

A special word of thanks is owed to Miss Lorraine Ourom and her colleagues at the University of Toronto Press for their kindly interest and helpful advice in the preparation of the typescript for offset reproduction.

If this revision proves of greater service in making students aware of the subtleties and richness of expression of the language of the Old Testament, the author will be amply rewarded.

R.J.W.
September 4, 1975

Contents

V SYNTAX OF CLAUSES

HEBREW SYNTAX: An Outline

Abbreviations

Am	Amos	KAI	Donner-Röllig, *Kanaan-äische und aramäische Inschriften*
Ca	Canticles		
Ch	Chronicles		
Da	Daniel	Kg	Kings
Dt	Deuteronomy	La	Lamentations
Ec	Ecclesiastes	Lv	Leviticus
Es	Esther	Mi	Micah
Ex	Exodus	Na	Nahum
Ez	Ezra	Ne	Nehemiah
Ezk	Ezekiel	Nu	Numbers
Gn	Genesis	Ob	Obadiah
Ho	Hosea	Pr	Proverbs
Is	Isaiah	Ps	Psalms
Jb	Job	Ru	Ruth
Je	Jeremiah	Si	Sirach
Jl	Joel	Sm	Samuel
Jn	Jonah	UTB	Gordon, *Ugaritic Textbook*
Jo	Joshua		
Ju	Judges	Zp	Zephaniah

<>   enclosing words in translations or Hebrew text
indicate a scribal omission

I Introduction

While the morphology and lexicon of Hebrew are reasonably well understood, its syntax was for long the most neglected area of study. Many examples may be cited from the Revised Standard Version to show that it is weak precisely at this point. Likewise, although many of the emendations proposed in the notes to Kittel's *Biblia Hebraica* reveal much ingenuity on the part of the editors, they all too frequently reveal a disregard for the principles of Hebrew syntax.

Syntax, the relationship of words to one another, forms together with morphology the material of grammar. Its relative importance varies according to the language considered. This is particularly true in the case of word order, and may be illustrated by languages as different structurally as Sanskrit and Chinese. The former, a highly inflected language, allows great freedom in the order of words, since case endings make the functions of words abundantly clear. On the other hand, Chinese has no inflections, and consequently the word order assumes a prime importance and becomes inflexible; position is the key to the understanding of a Chinese sentence. When an inflected language loses its case endings, as English did, then word order and the increased use of prepositions assume the functions of the former cases. That is why the two statements *the man hit the boy* and *the boy hit the man* have diametrically opposite meanings. Hebrew is in a similar position to English, having early lost its case endings, and so depending largely on position for grammatical function. It is unfortunate that the significance of word order in Hebrew has not been fully appreciated by grammarians.

The contents of this volume have been developed over the past fifteen years as a series of notes dictated to classes in a formal course on Hebrew syntax at the University of Toronto. This has determined both their form and their brevity. The work makes no claim to be an exhaustive study but, as the title implies, merely an outline for the use of advanced classes in biblical Hebrew.

Linguists may be dismayed by the fact that descriptions of syntactic functions are not exclusively intrinsic. That is to say, distinctions have sometimes been made by a comparison of the 'source language' (Hebrew) with the 'target language' (English). It is axiomatic that ideally only distinctions felt by native speakers of a language are valid. Nevertheless, years spent in teaching Hebrew to English-speaking students have shown the necessity of contrasting Hebrew usage with that of

3

English. For this reason, some further distinctions are desirable. There is, of course, no suggestion that the Hebrew speaker was conscious of the minute distinctions we have made. For instance, in making an utterance which required the use of the preposition לְ he most certainly would not ask himself which of the nineteen uses of this preposition was being employed! For the Hebrew student, however, a careful cataloguing of the various nuances of such a morpheme is of real value for a full appreciation of the range of meanings which it possesses.

This description is based on classical Hebrew prose, but some account is also taken of the deviations in later prose as well as in poetry. An important feature of the work is a selection of illustrative examples which should be carefully studied. All the citations have been taken from the third edition of Kittel's *Biblia Hebraica*. A complete listing of the passages cited will be found at the end. A selected index of Hebrew words will make it possible for the reader to find the main discussions of particles not listed in the Table of Contents. A detailed subject index concludes the volume. The references in the text and the indices are to the numbers of the paragraphs.

The final chapter treats of the syntax of clauses. In some cases readers may feel that the term 'sentence' would be more appropriate. The fact is that, although in Hebrew the features of juncture make the recognition of clauses an easy task, the problem of defining the limits of a Hebrew sentence is more difficult, and it is probably better to avoid the term.

Perhaps a word should be added concerning nomenclature. For the widely accepted terms 'absolute' and 'construct' I have adopted the more accurate linguistic expressions 'free form' and 'bound form,' the construction known as סְמִיכוּת being designated as 'bound structure,' following a suggestion of my colleague Professor J. W. Wevers. To describe the בִּנְיָנִים of the verb, I have preferred the designation 'theme' to the less accurate 'stem' which has a much wider connotation. Since biblical Hebrew had early abandoned the tense concept in favour of an aspectual one, the use of 'aspect' in place of 'tense' is desirable. To describe the verbal form contained in the construction usually known as '*waw*-consecutive plus imperfect,' the word 'preterite' has been chosen to indicate its original tense signification as well as the fact that its origin was different from that of the imperfect, as is shown by the weak verbs and the *Hip͏̄ʿil* of strong verbs. 'Precative' has been used for the independent verbal form commonly designated as 'jussive' or 'cohortative.' The latter expressions are restricted to certain persons of the verb, and a general term denoting the paradigm as a whole is preferable.

Finally, a word to describe verbal roots other than

stative is needed. Those in current use are either 'active' (properly to be contrasted with 'passive') or 'intransitive' (the opposite of 'transitive'; yet many statives have direct objects). The more appropriate designation 'fientive' has therefore been adopted.

II Syntax of the Noun

1 NUMBER

Singular

1 To indicate a single person or thing, e.g. מֶלֶךְ, 'a king,' מִזְבֵּחַ, 'an altar.'

2 To indicate collectives, e.g. עַם, 'people,' בָּקָר, 'cattle,' צֹאן, 'flocks'; note that עֵץ, 'a tree,' 'trees,' may be either a singular or a collective.

Dual

3 By the biblical period the dual had become obsolescent and restricted in its usage. It is confined to substantives, since adjectives and verbs are inflected for singular and plural only.

4 To indicate objects which occur naturally in pairs, e.g. יָדַיִם, 'hands,' אָזְנַיִם, 'ears,' נַעֲלַיִם, 'sandals' (however always זְרֹעִי or זְרֹעוֹת, 'arms'!), even when more than two are mentioned, e.g. שֵׁשׁ כְּנָפַיִם, 'six wings' (Is 6:2), אַרְבַּע רַגְלַיִם, 'four feet' (Lv 11:23).

5 To indicate two of a kind, e.g. מָאתַיִם, 'two hundred,' שְׁנָתַיִם, 'two years,' אַמָּתַיִם, 'two cubits,' יוֹמַיִם, 'two days.'

Plural

6 To indicate plurality, e.g. מְלָכִים, 'kings,' מִזְבְּחוֹת, 'altars.'

7 To indicate abstract ideas, e.g. בְּתוּלִים, 'virginity,' זְקֻנִים, 'old age,' נְעוּרִים, 'youth,' סַנְוֵרִים, 'blindness,' חַיִּים, 'life.'

8 To indicate respect, often with attributive adjectives in the singular, e.g. אֱלֹהִים חַי, 'the living God' (II Kg 19:4; but contrast אֱלֹהִים חַיִּים in I Sm 17:26), אֲדֹנִים קָשֶׁה,

6

'a harsh master' (Is 19:4), קֹבְרֹתֶיךָ, 'your grave' (II Kg 22:20).

9 To indicate composition, e.g. עֲפָרוֹת, 'lumps,' 'earth clods' (Pr 8:26, Jb 28:6), עֵצִים, 'timber,' 'firewood' (contrast §2; but note Is 7:2, Ps 96:12), כְּסָפִים, 'silver pieces' (Gn 42:25, 35).

10 To indicate natural products in an unnatural condition, e.g. חִטִּים, 'wheat' in grains (cf. חִטָּה in the ear), כֻּסְּמִים, 'spelt' (cf. כֻּסֶּמֶת), שְׂעֹרִים, 'barley' (cf. שְׂעֹרָה), דָּמִים, 'shed blood.'

11 Plural of extension, when the object consists of several parts, e.g. פָּנִים, 'face,' צַוָּארִים, 'neck,' שָׁמַיִם, 'sky,' 'heaven.'

Formation of Compound Plurals

12 By pluralizing the first element, e.g. גִּבּוֹרֵי חַיִל, 'valiant warriors' (I Ch 7:2), בְּנֵי יְמִינִי, 'Benjaminites' (I Sm 22:7).

13 By pluralizing both elements, e.g. גִּבּוֹרֵי חֲיָלִים, 'valiant warriors' (I Ch 7:5), שָׂרֵי הַחֲיָלִים, 'army commanders' (I Kg 15:20), בָּתֵּי כְלָאִים, 'prisons' (Is 42:22).

14 By pluralizing the second element only, e.g. בֵּית אָבוֹת, 'paternal estates,' 'families' (II Ch 25:5), בֵּית בָּמוֹת, 'high place sanctuaries' (I Kg 12:31).

Repetition

15 Distributive (cf. §100), e.g. יוֹם יוֹם, 'day after day' (Gn 39:10), אִישׁ אִישׁ, 'any person' (Lv 17:10), יוֹם לַשָּׁנָה יוֹם לַשָּׁנָה, 'one day for each year' (Nu 14:34).

16 Emphatic, e.g. אֲשֶׁר זָהָב זָהָב וַאֲשֶׁר־כֶּסֶף כֶּסֶף, 'which were of pure gold and silver' (II Kg 25:15), גֵּבִים גֵּבִים, 'nothing but trenches' (II Kg 3:16), מְעַט מְעַט, 'very gradually' (Ex 23:30), שָׁלוֹם שָׁלוֹם, 'perfect peace' (Is 26:3); cf. Gn 14:10, Nu 3:9, Dt 16:20.

7

2 GENDER

Masculine

17 To indicate the male sex, e.g. אָב, 'father,' מֶלֶךְ, 'king.'

18 To indicate grammatical gender for inanimate objects, e.g. בַּיִת, 'house,' דָּבָר, 'word,' 'thing,' לֵבָב, 'heart,' 'mind.'

19 In the plural to express abstract ideas (cf. §7), e.g. חַיִּים, 'life,' זְקֻנִים, 'old age.'

Feminine

20 To indicate the female sex, e.g. אֵם, 'mother,' מַלְכָּה, 'queen.'

21 To indicate grammatical gender for inanimate objects, e.g. חֶרֶב, 'sword,' כּוֹס, 'cup,' אֵשׁ, 'fire.'

22 Often to indicate parts of the body, especially those occurring in pairs, e.g. רֶגֶל, 'foot,' אֹזֶן, 'ear,' קֶרֶן, 'horn.'

23 Proper names of countries and cities are usually construed as feminine, e.g. מִצְרַיִם, 'Egypt' (Gn 41:8), מוֹאָב, 'Moab' (II Sm 8:2), צֹר, 'Tyre' (Ezk 26:2). When treated as masculine, they normally refer to the inhabitants, but contrast אֲרָם in II Sm 10:14 with II Sm 8:5.

24 To express abstract ideas, e.g. אֱמוּנָה, 'faithfulness,' אַהֲבָה, 'love,' גְּבוּרָה, 'strength,' טוֹבָה, 'welfare,' 'benefit.'

25 To express neuter concepts, e.g. זֹאת, 'this' (II Kg 3:18), נִפְלָאֹת, 'wonderful things' (Ex 34:10).

26 To form collectives, e.g. יוֹשֶׁבֶת, 'inhabitants,' אֹיֶבֶת, 'enemies,' אֹרְחָה, 'caravan.'

27 To indicate the single component of a collective, e.g. אֳנִיָּה, 'ship' (cf. אֳנִי, 'fleet'), שַׂעֲרָה, 'a hair' (cf. שֵׂעָר, 'hair').

3 BOUND STRUCTURE

28 Nouns may be combined into a single accentual unit where

the second element delimits the range of the first, e.g. דִּבְרֵי הַנְּבִיאִים, 'the prophets' words' (I Kg 22:13). The phonetic structure of the language normally results in reduction of vowels in the first component, which is a bound form. The second element, a free form, is in the genitive relationship (cf. §§31, 36), so that the construction is comparable to that in modern Welsh *geiriau y proffwydi*, 'the prophets' words,' where the original case endings have likewise fallen away.

29 The bound form should be anarthrous, but note Phoenician הברך בעל, 'blessed of Baal' (KAI, 26A 1:1) and Hebrew וְאֵת כָּל־הַמַּמְלְכוֹת הָאָרֶץ, 'and all the kingdoms of the earth' (Je 25:26); cf. Ju 8:11, Jo 3:14, I Kg 14:24, II Kg 23: 17 (twice), 25:19. It should also directly precede its genitive, except when two genitives are closely related, e.g. אֵם יַעֲקֹב וְעֵשָׂו, 'the mother of Jacob and Esau' (Gn 28:5); cf. Dt 10:18, Gn 14:19. Only one bound form may precede the same genitive; exceptional are the late expressions סֵפֶר וּלְשׁוֹן כַּשְׂדִּים, 'the writings and language of the Chaldeans' (Da 1:4) and מִבְחַר וְטוֹב־לְבָנוֹן, 'the choicest and best of Lebanon' (Ezk 31:16).

30 However, the Directive הָ may intervene in a bound structure (cf. §62). Occasionally a bound form occurs before prepositions, e.g. מַשְׁכִּימֵי בַבֹּקֶר, 'early morning risers' (Is 5:11); cf. I Sm 9:3, I Kg 22:13, II Sm 1:21, Ju 5: 10. Rarely the bound form of a substantive is followed by an adjective (cf. §42), e.g. כְּלִי הַקָּטֹן, 'the small vessels' (Is 22:24); cf. Is 28:4, 16. The second element of a bound structure may also be a noun clause (cf. §489), e.g. כָּל־יְמֵי הִתְהַלַּכְנוּ אִתָּם, 'all the days we went about with them' (I Sm 25:15). Some curious instances of hypallage (inversion of syntactical relationships) should be noted, e.g. כָּל־עוֹד נַפְשִׁי בִּי, 'my whole life is still in me' (II Sm 1:9); cf. Jb 27:3, Is 19:8, Ho 14:3.

9

4 CASE

31 The short vowels of the original case endings, preserved
in Ugaritic, Akkadian and classical Arabic, were lost in
Hebrew *ca*. 1000 B.C. It is thus strictly speaking incor-
rect to speak of cases in Hebrew. However, the names of
the three cases may be conveniently employed to designate
those syntactic functions of nouns which would have been
indicated by the appropriate case endings in an earlier
period. That biblical Hebrew was still aware of these
separate functions is clear from the use of the particle
אֵת before nouns in all situations which would require an
accusative case ending (cf. §475).

Nominative

32 Subject of a sentence, e.g. הַנָּחָשׁ הִשִּׁיאַנִי, 'the serpent
has deluded me' (Gn 3:13) and *passim*.

33 Predicative noun, which is regularly anarthrous, e.g.
כִּי־גֵרִים הֱיִיתֶם בְּאֶרֶץ מִצְרָיִם, 'for you were aliens in the
land of Egypt' (Dt 10:19); cf. Jo 2:17. When the article
is present it expresses the superlative (cf. §93), e.g.
כִּי אַתֶּם הָרַבִּים, 'for you are the more numerous' (I Kg 18:
25); cf. I Sm 9:21; or is the distinctive use of the article (cf. §88), e.g. הַצַּדִּיק וַאֲנִי וְעַמִּי הָרְשָׁעִים יְ', 'the
righteous one is Yahweh, while the guilty ones are I and
my people' (Ex 9:27).

34 Vocative, regularly with the article (cf. §89), e.g.
וַתֹּאמֶר הוֹשִׁעָה הַמֶּלֶךְ, 'She said, "Give aid, O king!"' (II
Sm 14:4).

35 Rhetorical absolute (*casus pendens*), a nominative case
in exposed position resumed by a later word (cf. §573),
e.g. הַמָּקוֹם in Dt 12:11 or הָאָרֶץ in Dt 11:10.

Genitive

36 This designates the grammatical function which occurs
after bound forms, including prepositions.

10

37 Subjective, e.g. דְּבַר־יְהוָה, 'Yahweh's word' (Je 1:2), חָכְמַת שְׁלֹמֹה, 'Solomon's wisdom' (I Kg 5:10), אַהֲבַת יְהוָה, 'Yahweh's love' (I Kg 10:9).

38 Objective, e.g. אֶרֶץ זָבַת חָלָב וּדְבָשׁ, 'a land flowing with milk and honey' (Dt 6:3), חֲמַס אָחִיךָ, 'the violence done to your brother' (Ob 10).

39 Possessive, e.g. בֵּית הַמֶּלֶךְ, 'the king's house' (I Kg 9: 10), הֵיכַל יְהוָה, 'Yahweh's temple' (Je 7:4).

40 Material, e.g. כְּלֵי כֶסֶף, 'silver vessels' (I Kg 10:25), אֲרוֹן עֵץ, 'a wooden ark' (Dt 10:1); so with numerals (cf. §95), e.g. שְׁלֹשֶׁת יָמִים, 'three days' (Gn 30:36).

41 Attributive, where English would employ an adjective, e.g. גִּבּוֹר חַיִל, 'an affluent man' (I Sm 9:1), מֹאזְנֵי צֶדֶק, 'just scales' (Lv 19:36), הַר־קָדְשִׁי, 'my holy mountain' (Ps 2:6).

42 Appositional, e.g. אֶרֶץ מִצְרַיִם, 'the land of Egypt' (Ex 7:19), נְהַר־פְּרָת, 'the river Euphrates' (Gn 15:18), בַּת צִיּוֹן, 'the daughter Zion' (II Kg 19:21), אֵשֶׁת בַּעֲלַת־אוֹב, 'a wo- man who has a familiar spirit' (I Sm 28:7); cf. Ju 19: 22. It occurs also with adjectives, e.g. בַּשָּׁנָה הַתְּשִׁיעִית, 'in the ninth year' (II Kg 17:6), עֹלַת הַתָּמִיד, 'the regu- lar burnt offering' (Nu 28:31).

43 Explicative, e.g. עֲצֵי שִׁטִּים, 'acacia wood' (Ex 37:10), אַבְנֵי־שַׁיִשׁ, 'marble stone' (I Ch 29:2).

44 Result, e.g. צֹאן טִבְחָה, 'sheep for slaughter' (Ps 44:23, with which contrast צֹאן לְטִבְחָה in Je 12:3 and §279), מוּסַר שְׁלוֹמֵנוּ, 'chastisement for our welfare' (Is 53:5).

45 Agent or means, after the bound form of a passive par- ticiple, e.g. מֻכֵּה אֱלֹהִים, 'smitten by God' (Is 53:4), שְׂרֻפוֹת אֵשׁ, 'burned with fire' (Is 1:7).

46 Specification or epexegetical, after the bound form of an adjective, e.g. קְשֵׁה־עֹרֶף, 'stiff-necked' (Ex 32:9), יְפֵה־תֹאַר, 'fair of form,' 'handsome' (Gn 39:6).

47 Superlative, e.g. שִׁיר הַשִּׁירִים, 'the finest song' (Ca 1:1), אֱלֹהֵי הָאֱלֹהִים, 'the supreme God' (Dt 10:17); cf. Ex 29:37.

11

48　Measure or number (rare), e.g. מְתֵי מִסְפָּר, 'a few men' (Gn 34:30), מֵי מָתְנָיִם, 'water up to the thighs' (Ezk 47:4); contrast §69.

49　Dependent, after prepositions: *passim*.

Accusative

50　Direct object of a verb, e.g. וַיִּבְרָא אֱלֹהִים אֶת־הָאָדָם, 'God created mankind' (Gn 1:27) and *passim*.

51　Cognate accusative, e.g. פָּחֲדוּ פָחַד, 'they were in sheer terror' (Ps 14:5), חֵטְא חָטְאָה יְרוּשָׁלַם, 'Jerusalem committed a great sin' (La 1:8); cf. II Kg 4:13, 13:14.

52　Product or result, e.g. וַיִּבְנֶה אֶת־הָאֲבָנִים מִזְבֵּחַ, 'he built the stones into an altar' (I Kg 18:32); cf. I Sm 8:1.

53　Of material, e.g. וַיִּרְגְּמוּ אֹתוֹ כָל־יִשְׂרָאֵל אֶבֶן, 'all Israel stoned him with stones' (Jo 7:25), וַיִּיצֶר יְ' אֱלֹהִים אֶת־הָאָדָם עָפָר, 'Yahweh God formed mankind of dust' (Gn 2:7); cf. Dt 27:6.

54　Directive or terminative, after verbs of motion, e.g. וְצֵא הַשָּׂדֶה, 'go out to the field' (Gn 27:3). The apparent exceptions בֵּית (e.g. II Kg 19:37) and פֶּתַח (e.g. II Kg 5: 9) are really bound forms of substantives used locatively as prepositions (probably in the accusative of manner, cf. §60), similarly to דֶּרֶךְ, 'towards,' מוּל, 'opposite,' אֵצֶל, 'beside' (Dt 11:30).

55　Separative, only after יָצָא, e.g. בָּנַי יְצָאֻנִי וְאֵינָם, 'my sons have gone from me and are no more' (Je 10:20); cf. Gn 44:4, Am 4:3.

56　Temporal, expressing duration of time, e.g. כָּל־יְמֵי חַיֶּיךָ, 'all the days of your life' (Gn 3:14); cf. Ex 13:7 (N.B. אֵת), Dt 9:25. Contrast וּשְׁתַּיִם שָׁנִים מָלַךְ, 'and he reigned for two years' (II Sm 2:10) with וַיָּבֹאוּ אֵלָיו בַּשָּׁנָה הַשֵּׁנִית, 'they came to him in the second year' (Gn 47:18), וַיְשַׁלְּחֵם לַיְלָה, 'he dispatched them during the night' (Jo 8:3) with וַיֵּרָא אֵלָיו יְ' בַּלַּיְלָה הַהוּא, 'Yahweh appeared to him on that night' (Gn 26:24) and הַלַּיְלָה with בַּבֹּקֶר in Ru 3:13.

57　Of specification, e.g. חָלָה אֶת־רַגְלָיו, 'he suffered in his

12

feet' (I Kg 15:23), לֹא נַכֶּנּוּ נָפֶשׁ, 'let us not wound him mortally,' lit. 'with respect to life' (Gn 37:21); cf. Gn 41:40, II Sm 15:32. This may occasionally be a clause (cf. §492). Here belongs the predicative accusative (contrast the predicative nominative, §33) which is anarthrous, e.g. וַיִּשְׁמַע מֹשֶׁה אֶת־הָעָם בֹּכֶה, 'Moses heard the people weeping' (Nu 11:10), אֹתְךָ רָאִיתִי צַדִּיק, 'I have seen you to be righteous' (Gn 7:1); cf. I Sm 9:11.

58 Emphatic accusative of specification, an instance of prolepsis in which the accusative is the semantic subject preceding the verb which exhibits concord of person, number and gender, e.g. יָדַעְתָּ אֶת־אַבְנֵר בֶּן־נֵר כִּי לְפַתֹּתְךָ בָּא, 'you know that Abner ben Ner came to deceive you' (II Sm 3:25), וַיִּרְאוּ הַמִּצְרִים אֶת־הָאִשָּׁה כִּי־יָפָה הִוא מְאֹד, 'the Egyptians saw that the woman was very beautiful' (Gn 12:14); cf. I Kg 5:17, Gn 1:4. Sometimes no verb precedes, e.g. וְאֶת־הַבַּרְזֶל נָפַל אֶל־הַמָּיִם, 'the iron (axe head) fell into the water' (II Kg 6:5); cf. Nu 11:22 (here the following verb is singular!), Ju 6:28, II Sm 21:22. In place of a finite verb, it may be followed by a construct infinitive, e.g. וַיִּשְׁאַל אֶת־נַפְשׁוֹ לָמוּת, 'he requested that his life might end,' lit. 'die' (I Kg 19:4; contrast I Kg 19:10). This differs only slightly from the rhetorical absolute (cf. §35); note the example וְאִישׁ אֶת־קֳדָשָׁיו לוֹ יִהְיוּ, 'as for anyone, in the matter of his sacred things, they shall be his' (Nu 5:10), where אִישׁ is a rhetorical absolute and אֶת־קֳ' an emphatic accusative of specification.

59 Determinative, in which the apparent object is really the subject and follows the verb without concord, since it is impersonal and often passive, e.g. וַיֻּגַּד לְרִבְקָה אֶת־דִּבְרֵי עֵשָׂו, 'Esau's words were told to Rebekah' (Gn 27:42); cf. Gn 17:5, Am 4:2, Dt 12:22, I Kg 2:21, II Sm 11:25, Ne 9:32, I Sm 20:13, and medieval Latin *legitur Vergilium*, 'Vergil is read.' This may also occur with an in-

finitive, e.g. בְּהִוָּלֶד לוֹ אֵת יִצְחָק בְּנוֹ, 'when his son Isaac was born to him' (Gn 21:5); cf. Gn 21:8, Nu 7:10. Sometimes a clause is the subject (cf. §493), e.g. הֻגֵּד הֻגַּד לַעֲבָדֶיךָ אֵת אֲשֶׁר צִוָּה יּ, 'your servants were clearly told that Yahweh had commanded' (Jo 9:24). Exceptions, in which the verb exhibits concord, are Nu 17:2f., II Kg 18:30 (=Is 36:15) and Gn 29:27. In הַמְעַט־לָנוּ אֶת־עֲוֺן פְּעוֹר, 'Was the offence at Peor so insignificant for us?' (Jo 22:17) the predicate is not a verb but an adjective.

60 Manner is expressed by the accusative, also known as the adverbial accusative. It is anarthrous, e.g. וַתֵּשְׁבוּ בֶּטַח, 'you lived in security' (I Sm 12:11), קוֹמְמִיּוּת, 'erect' (Lv 26:13); cf. I Sm 13:17; so also in the case of מְאֹד, 'very,' הַרְבֵּה, 'much,' etc. This may even, on occasion, be a clause (cf. §491).

5 DIRECTIVE הָ‍

61 That this is not the old accusative ending is clear from the evidence of Ugaritic, in which arṣh = אַרְצָה and šmmh = הַשָּׁמַיְמָה. However, this ending is not present in שָׁמָּה, Ugaritic ṯmt, where the ending is an original deictic t as in Ugaritic hmt = הֵמָּה; cf. II Kg 23:8.

62 Directive or terminative, e.g. הַבֶּט־נָא הַשָּׁמַיְמָה, 'just look at the sky' (Gn 15:5), הָבֵא אֶת־הָאֲנָשִׁים הַבָּיְתָה, 'bring the men into the house' (Gn 43:16). This ending may intervene between a bound form and its genitive (cf. §30), e.g. בֵּיתָה יוֹסֵף, 'into Joseph's house' (Gn 43:17), מִדְבָּרָה דַמֶּשֶׂק, 'towards the wilderness of Damascus' (I Kg 19:15).

63 Temporal, meaning 'until,' e.g. מִיָּמִים יָמִימָה, 'from year to year' (Ex 13:10, Ju 11:40).

64 Sometimes separative with מִן, e.g. מִבָּבֶלָה, 'from Babylon' (Je 27:16), מִצָּפוֹנָה, 'from/on the north' (Jo 15:10). Note the irregular use with בְּ, e.g. I Sm 23:15, 18f., 31:13, II Sm 20:15, or אֵצֶל, e.g. I Kg 4:12 (all proper names!).

14

65 Genus and species, e.g. אִשָּׁה אַלְמָנָה, 'a widow woman' (I Kg
7:14), נַעֲרָה בְתוּלָה, 'a virgin lass' (I Kg 1:2), אִישׁ כֹּהֵן,
'a priest' (Lv 21:9).

66 Attributive, in which the second element is equivalent
to an adjective (contrast §41), e.g. אֲמָרִים אֱמֶת, 'true
words' (Pr 22:21), יַיִן תַּרְעֵלָה, 'intoxicating wine,' lit.
'wine, staggering' (Ps 60:5), לָשׁוֹן רְמִיָּה, 'a deceitful
tongue' (Ps 120:3).

67 Predicative, in which a substantive is used in place of
an adjective (cf. §562), e.g. הֲשָׁלוֹם אֲבִיכֶם הַזָּקֵן, 'is your
old father well?' (Gn 43:27), אֱמֶת הָיָה הַדָּבָר, 'the report
was true' (I Kg 10:6).

68 Material, e.g. סְאָה־סֹלֶת, 'a measure of flour' (II Kg 7:1),
הַבָּקָר הַנְּחֹשֶׁת, 'the bronze oxen' (II Kg 16:17), שְׁנָתַיִם יָמִים,
'two full years' (Gn 41:1); cf. Ex 39:17, II Kg 3:4, 5:
17, I Ch 15:19. So with numerals, e.g. שְׁלֹשָׁה בָנִים, 'three
sons' (Gn 6:10; contrast §40). Occasionally the first
element has the article while the second is anarthrous,
e.g. הַמַּבּוּל מַיִם, 'the flood waters' (Gn 6:17); cf. Phoenician המזבח נחשת זן, 'this bronze altar' (KAI, 10:4).

69 Measure or number, e.g. יָמִים מִסְפָּר, 'a few days' (Nu 9:
20), מַיִם בִּרְכַּיִם, 'water extending to the knees' (Ezk 47:
4); contrast §48.

70 Explicative, giving the name or title (contrast §42),
e.g. הָאָרֶץ כְּנַעַן, 'the land of Canaan' (Nu 34:2), לִשְׁלֹמֹה
הַמֶּלֶךְ, 'to King Solomon' (I Kg 2:17), the former being
the commoner order. When the name follows, any preposition or the accusative particle is repeated, e.g. Gn 24:
4, 4:2 (but note the exceptions in Gn 24:12, I Sm 25:19,
Jb 1:8), whereas when the name precedes this is not so,
e.g. Gn 4:8, 16:3.

71 Anticipative, with pronominal suffixes. This is common
in Aramaic and Ethiopic, but rare in Hebrew, e.g. וַתִּרְאֵהוּ
אֶת־הַיֶּלֶד, 'she saw the lad' (Ex 2:6), בְּבֹאוֹ הָאִישׁ, 'when

the man entered' (Ezk 10:3); cf. I Kg 21:13.

7 HENDIADYS

72 A single concept may be expressed by two words linked
by the conjunction וְ, e.g. חָמָס וָשֹׁד (Am 3:10, Je 6:7, 20:
8, Ezk 45:9), cf. 'assault and battery'; נִין וָנֶכֶד (Is
14:22, Gn 21:23, Jb 18:19), cf. 'kith and kin'; חֶסֶד וֶאֱמֶת,
'true loyalty' (Ex 34:6, Jo 2:14, II Sm 2:6, 15:20; it
is significant that in Pr 16:6 only one preposition is
used); הַבְּרִית וְהַחֶסֶד, 'the loyal covenant' (Dt 7:9, 12,
I Kg 8:23, Ne 9:32); הוֹד וְהָדָר, 'glorious splendour' (Jb
40:10); חֹשֶׁךְ וְצַלְמָוֶת, 'blackest darkness' (Jb 10:21); תֹּהוּ
וָבֹהוּ, 'a formless void' (Gn 1:2); דְּמָמָה וָקוֹל, 'a whisper-
ing voice' (Jb 4:16); עִצְּבוֹנֵךְ וְהֵרֹנֵךְ, 'your labour pains'
(Gn 3:16).

8 ADJECTIVES

73 Attributive adjectives follow their substantives, with
concord of gender, number and determination, e.g. אֱלֹהִים
אֲחֵרִים, 'alien gods' (Dt 8:19) and בִּתִּי הַגְּדוֹלָה, 'my older
daughter' (I Sm 18:17). However, with dual substantives
the plural is used, e.g. בִּרְכַּיִם כֹּרְעוֹת, 'tottering knees'
(Jb 4:4). This may also occur with collectives, e.g. הָעָם
הַנִּמְצָאִים עִמּוֹ, 'the people present with him' (I Sm 13:15);
cf. Gn 30:36. Plurals of respect may be accompanied by
singular or plural adjectives (cf. §8). Attributive adjectives follow all the constituent elements of a bound
structure, showing concord with the component to which
they refer, e.g. בִּגְדֵי עֵשָׂו בְּנָהּ הַגָּדֹל הַחֲמֻדֹת, 'the best clothing of her older son Esau' (Gn 27:15). Anomalous instances of an anarthrous substantive with a determinated
adjective do occur, e.g. חָצֵר הַגְּדוֹלָה, 'the great court'
(I Kg 7:12); cf. Ezk 40:28, Je 6:20, I Sm 12:23.

74 Demonstrative adjectives follow their substantives and

any attributive adjectives (exceptional are Je 13:10, II Ch 1:10), with concord of gender, number and determination, e.g. הַמִּשְׁפָּחָה הָרָעָה הַזֹּאת, 'this wicked clan' (Je 8:3), בַּיָּמִים הָרַבִּים הָהֵם, 'within those many days' (Ex 2:23); but note בַּלַּיְלָה הוּא, 'on that night,' in Gn 19:33, 30:16, 32:23, I Sm 19:10. However, they do not take the article when modifying a substantive made definite by reason of a pronominal suffix, but are used in apposition, e.g. לֵךְ בְּכֹחֲךָ זֶה, 'Go in this strength of yours' (Ju 6:14); cf. Dt 5:29, Jo 2:20, II Kg 1:13, Gn 24:8; but Jo 2:17 and II Ch 1:10 are anomalies.

75 Predicate adjectives in non-verbal clauses normally precede their substantives with concord of gender and number, but are regularly anarthrous (cf. §33), e.g. רַבָּה רָעַת הָאָדָם, 'the wickedness of mankind was great' (Gn 6:5) and רַבִּים רַחֲמָיו, 'his compassion is great' (I Ch 21:13). Only very rarely do they fail to exhibit concord, e.g. יָשָׁר מִשְׁפָּטֶיךָ, 'your judgments are upright' (Ps 119:137). When in circumstantial (cf. §494) and subordinate clauses they follow the subject, e.g. וּבְנֵי יִשְׂרָאֵל יֹצְאִים, 'as the Israelites went forth' (Ex 14:8), כִּי הַמָּקוֹם קָדֹשׁ, 'because the place is holy' (Ezk 42:13).

76 Comparison is expressed by מִן (cf. §§317f.), e.g. גָּבֹהַּ מִכָּל־הָעָם, 'taller than all the people' (I Sm 9:2), כִּי־הָיָה רְכוּשָׁם רָב מִשֶּׁבֶת יַחְדָּו, 'their possessions were too great for them to live together' (Gn 36:7); cf. I Kg 8:64.

77 The superlative may be expressed in several ways:
- By means of a determinated adjective, e.g. בְּנוֹ הַקָּטָן, 'his youngest son' (Gn 9:24); cf. §93.

78 - By employing a bound structure, e.g. קְטֹן בָּנָיו, 'the youngest of his sons' (II Ch 21:17).

79 - By means of a pronominal suffix, e.g. טוֹבָם, 'the best of them' (Mi 7:4), מִגְּדוֹלָם וְעַד־קְטַנָּם, 'from the greatest of them to the least of them' (Jn 3:5).

80 - By means of a superlative genitive (cf. §47), e.g. עֶבֶד

17

עֲבָדִים, 'an abject slave' (Gn 9:25), הֶבֶל הֲבָלִים, 'utter vanity/futility' (Ec 1:2).

81 - By using a divine epithet, e.g. עִיר־גְּדוֹלָה לֵאלֹהִים, 'an exceedingly great city' (Jn 3:3), וַתְּהִי לְחֶרְדַּת אֱלֹהִים, 'it became a terrible panic' (I Sm 14:15); cf. Gn 35:5, I Sm 11:7, Ps 80:11, 36:7. So also in Ugaritic, e.g. ṯlḥn. ỉl, 'a wonderful table' (UTB, 51.i.39).

9   THE ARTICLE

82 The article is regularly omitted from bound forms and substantives with pronominal suffixes (but cf. §29 and note the anomalous forms in Gn 31:13, Ex 9:18, Lv 27:23, Jo 7:21, 8:33, II Kg 15:16, 23:17, Is 36:16, Ezk 46:19, Ps 123:4. This is not, of course, true of participles with the relative article (cf. §90), e.g. הַמַּאֲכִלְךָ מָן, 'who fed you manna' (Dt 8:16); cf. Dt 20:1, Ju 8:11, Is 9:12, Ps 18:33. The article is rare in poetry which, being somewhat archaic in its language, reflects the period before the development of the article, e.g. קֹנֵה שָׁמַיִם וָאָרֶץ, 'the creator of sky and earth' (Gn 14:19).

83 To indicate definiteness when the person or object has already been mentioned, e.g. וַיֹּאמֶר הַמֶּלֶךְ קְחוּ לִי־חָרֶב וַיָּבִאוּ הַחֶרֶב לִפְנֵי הַמֶּלֶךְ, 'The king said, "Fetch me a sword," so they brought the sword to the king' (I Kg 3:24); cf. Gn 18:7f.

84 The article is employed when the object or person is definite in the thought of the narrator, though such words are indefinite in English, e.g. בַּסֵּפֶר, 'on a scroll' (I Sm 10:25), or, introducing a story, וַיְהִי הַיּוֹם, 'a certain day,' 'one day' (II Kg 4:8); cf. I Sm 9:9, Jo 2:15.

85 As in English, the article is used when an object or a person is a well-known or recognized fact, e.g. וַיִּקַּח אַבְרָהָם אֶת־עֲצֵי הָעֹלָה . . . וַיִּקַּח בְּיָדוֹ אֶת־הָאֵשׁ וְאֶת־הַמַּאֲכֶלֶת, 'Abraham took the wood for the burnt offering . . . and took the fire and the knife in his hand' (Gn 22:6); cf.

II Sm 18:24.

86 Possessive, equivalent to a pronominal suffix, e.g. וְלָקַח דָּוִד אֶת־הַכִּנּוֹר, 'David would take his lyre' (I Sm 16:23); cf. Gn 24:65.

87 Demonstrative, e.g. הַפַּעַם, 'this time' (Gn 2:23), הַיּוֹם, 'today' (I Sm 24:19).

88 Distinctive, e.g. הָאֱלֹהִים, 'the true God' (I Kg 18:39), הַנָּהָר, 'the Euphrates' (Gn 31:21).

89 Vocative (cf. §34), e.g. הוֹשִׁיעָה אֲדֹנִי הַמֶּלֶךְ, 'Give aid, my lord king!' (II Kg 6:26).

90 Relative, i.e. equivalent to a relative pronoun:
- With participles (cf. §218), e.g. י' הַנִּרְאֶה אֵלָיו, 'Yahweh who had appeared to him' (Gn 12:7); cf. II Kg 22:18.

91 - With a perfect aspect, e.g. וְכֹל הַהִקְדִּישׁ שְׁמוּאֵל, 'and all that Samuel had dedicated' (I Ch 26:28), הַהֹלְכוּא אִתּוֹ, 'who had accompanied him' (Jo 10:24); cf. I Kg 11:9, Ez 8:25, 10:14, 17.

92 Generic, to express classes, e.g. הַכֶּלֶב, 'a dog' (Ju 7: 5), הָעֹרֵב, 'a raven' (Gn 8:7), הַכְּנַעֲנִי, 'the Canaanites' (Ju 1:1), הַצַּדִּיק, 'the righteous' (Ec 3:17); cf. II Kg 5: 27, I Sm 9:9, 17:34, Am 5:19. This is the normal use in comparisons, e.g. אֲדֻמִּים כַּדָּם, 'red as blood' (II Kg 3:22).

93 Superlative (cf. §77), e.g. כִּי־אַתֶּם הַמְעַט מִכָּל־הָעַמִּים, 'for you are the least of all the nations' (Dt 7:7), וּרְאִיתֶם הַטּוֹב וְהַיָּשָׁר מִבְּנֵי אֲדֹנֵיכֶם, 'Look for the best and the most upright of your master's sons' (II Kg 10:3).

10 NUMERALS

<u>Cardinal</u>

94 'One' is an attributive adjective (cf. §73), e.g. אִישׁ אֶחָד, 'one man' (Ju 18:19), אִשָּׁה אַחַת, 'a certain woman' (II Kg 4:1), הַמַּחֲנֶה הָאַחַת, 'the one camp' (Gn 32:9). Sometimes אֶחָד is anarthrous, even when its substantive is determinated, e.g. הָרֹאשׁ אֶחָד, 'the one band' (I Sm 13: 17f.).

19

95 'Two' to 'ten' are substantives which may precede a numbered object in the bound structure, the object being
in the plural of the genitive of material (cf. §40), or
may be in the free form with the object as an apposition of material (cf. §68), in neither case with concord
of gender (except for 'two'), e.g. חֲמֵשֶׁת מַלְכֵי מִדְיָן, 'the
five kings of Midian' (Nu 31:8) or וַחֲמִשָּׁה אֲנָשִׁים, 'five
men' (II Kg 25:19), וַחֲמֵשׁ מֵאוֹת, 'five hundred' (Jb 1:3)
or וְחָמֵשׁ נַעֲרֹתֶיהָ, 'her five maids' (I Sm 25:42), later
also אַמּוֹת חָמֵשׁ, 'five cubits' (II Ch 3:11); but שְׁנֵי אֲנָשִׁים,
'two men' (II Sm 4:2), שְׁתֵּי נָשִׁים, 'two women' (I Ch 4:5);
cf. שִׁבְעָה בָנִים וְשָׁלוֹשׁ בָּנוֹת, 'seven sons and three daughters' (Jb 1:2). For exceptions to the rule with regard
to gender see Gn 7:13, I Sm 10:3, Jb 1:4.

96 '11-19' and multiples of ten are substantives which normally precede in apposition to the object enumerated
which is in the plural (except, after '11-19,' for a few
common words, viz. אִישׁ, נֶפֶשׁ, שֶׁקֶל, שָׁנָה, יוֹם), the digit
showing inversion of gender, e.g. חֲמִשָּׁה עָשָׂר בָּנִים, 'fifteen sons' (II Sm 9:10); cf. Jo 4:8. Multiples of ten,
when preceding, require the enumerated object in the
plural, e.g. אַרְבָּעִים בָּנִים, 'forty sons' (Ju 12:14), except for the common words שֶׁקֶל, נֶפֶשׁ, שָׁנָה, יוֹם, אִישׁ, אֶלֶף
and פֹּר (cf. II Sm 15:1). When the numbered object precedes, the plural is always used, e.g. כֶּסֶף־שְׁקָלִים אַרְבָּעִים,
'forty shekels of silver' (Ne 5:15). When the expression
is definite the article may be prefixed either to the
numeral, e.g. שְׁנֵים הֶעָשָׂר אִישׁ, 'the twelve men' (Jo 4:4),
or to the accompanying substantive, e.g. אֶלֶף וּמֵאָה הַכֶּסֶף,
'the eleven hundred (shekels of) silver' (Ju 17:2); cf.
Jo 4:20, Gn 18:28.

97 Multiples of ten plus units have the enumerated object
either after, in the singular, e.g. שְׁתַּיִם וְשִׁשִּׁים שָׁנָה, 'sixty-two years' (Gn 5:20), or before, in the plural, e.g.
וְאַחֲרֵי הַשָּׁבֻעִים שִׁשִּׁים וּשְׁנַיִם, 'after the sixty-two weeks'

20

(Da 9:26). Note also the construction חָמֵשׁ שָׁנִים וְשִׁבְעִים שָׁנָה, 'seventy-five years' (Gn 12:4). The article may be prefixed to the numerals, e.g. הַשְּׁלֹשָׁה וְהַשִּׁבְעִים וְהַמָּאתָיִם, 'the two hundred and seventy-three' (Nu 3:46) or the accompanying substantive, e.g. Da 9:26 above.

Ordinal

98   'First' to 'tenth' are attributive adjectives (cf. §73), e.g. בַּשָּׁנָה הַשֵּׁנִית, 'in the second year' (Gn 47:18). Occasionally they occur after the bound form of the thing numbered, e.g. יוֹם הַשְּׁבִיעִי, 'the seventh day' (Dt 5:14); cf. II Kg 17:6. This is the appositional genitive (cf. §42). Rarely the bound form of a substantive is followed by a cardinal numeral, e.g. בִּשְׁנַת שְׁתַּיִם, 'in the second year' (II Kg 15:32); cf. II Kg 18:10. Sometimes a cardinal numeral is used for 'first,' e.g. . . . שֵׁם הָאֶחָד וְשֵׁם הַשֵּׁנִי, 'the name of the first . . ., while the name of the second' (II Sm 4:2).

99   'Eleventh,' etc. The cardinal numerals are employed, e.g. בְּשִׁבְעָה־עָשָׂר יוֹם, 'on the seventeenth day' (Gn 7:11), בִּשְׁנַת עֶשְׂרִים וָשֶׁבַע, 'in the twenty-seventh year' (I Kg 16:10), the enumerated object being anarthrous. When the expression is definite, the article may be attached to the numeral, e.g. וְהוּא בִּשְׁנֵים הֶעָשָׂר, 'he being with the twelfth' (I Kg 19:19), and exceptionally הַשְּׁנֵים עָשָׂר, 'the twelfth' (I Ch 25:19), although it may be omitted, e.g. בְּאַרְבָּעִים שָׁנָה בְּעַשְׁתֵּי־עָשָׂר חֹדֶשׁ, 'in the fortieth year, the eleventh month' (Dt 1:3).

Distributive

100   By simple repetition (cf. §15), e.g. שְׁנַיִם שְׁנַיִם, 'two by two' (Gn 7:9, 15) or בַּבֹּקֶר בַּבֹּקֶר, 'every morning' (Ex 30:7).

101   Repetition with the conjunction וְ (cf. §442), e.g. דּוֹר וָדוֹר, 'every generation' (Dt 32:7), שֵׁשׁ וָשֵׁשׁ, 'six each' (II Sm 21:20).

21

102 Repetition with the preposition בְּ (cf. §254), e.g. חֶדֶר
בְּחֶדֶר, 'room by room' (I Kg 20:30), כְּשָׁנָה בְשָׁנָה, 'as every
year' (II Kg 17:4); cf. I Sm 1:7, I Ch 12:23.

103 By employing the preposition לְ (cf. §281), e.g. לְמֵאוֹת
וְלַאֲלָפִים, 'by hundreds and thousands' (I Sm 29:2); cf.
Am 4:4.

104 Sometimes a word (usually a participle) occurs in the
plural with a singular predicate expressing the meaning
'everyone who,' e.g. וְתֹמְכֶיהָ מְאֻשָּׁר, 'everyone who holds
on to her is fortunate' (Pr 3:18), מְחַלְלֶיהָ מוֹת יוּמָת,
'everyone who profanes it will certainly be put to death'
(Ex 31:14); cf. Gn 27:29, Lv 17:14.

105 The substantive כֹּל followed by an indefinite substantive
may have a distributive sense, e.g. סֻגַּר כָּל־בַּיִת מִבּוֹא,
'every house is barred from entry' (Is 24:10); cf. Gn
2:9, Ru 4:7.

11 PRONOUNS

Independent Personal

106 As the subject of a finite verb for emphasis or contrast,
e.g. וְאַתָּה תִּמְשָׁל־בּוֹ, 'you are the one who must master it'
(Gn 4:7); cf. Dt 5:31.

107 In apposition to a pronominal suffix (in genitive or ac-
cusative functions), e.g. בָּרְכֵנִי גַם־אָנִי, 'Bless me too!'
(Gn 27:34), מִי־יִתֵּן מוּתִי אֲנִי, 'If only I myself had died!'
(II Sm 19:1), כִּי אִתָּנוּ אֲנַחְנוּ, 'but with us ourselves'
(Dt 5:3); cf. I Kg 21:19, II Sm 17:5. As a rhetorical
absolute (cf. §35) in the following: גַם אָנֹכִי חָלִילָה לִּי,
'Far be it from me too!' (I Sm 12:23).

108 As subject of a participle, e.g. אָנֹכִי מְצַוְּךָ הַיּוֹם, 'I am
commanding you today' (Dt 8:1), or a non-verbal clause,
e.g. אַתֶּם עַם־קְשֵׁה־עֹרֶף, 'You are a stiff-necked people'
(Ex 33:5).

22

Suffixed Personal

109 Subjective, e.g. אָכָלְכֶם, 'your eating' (Gn 3:5), בְּהִבָּרְאָם, 'when they were created' (Gn 2:4), לְבִלְתִּי עָבְרִי, 'that I should not cross' (Dt 4:21).

110 Objective, e.g. וַיַּנִּחֵהוּ . . . לְעָבְדָהּ, 'He put him . . . to till it' (Gn 2:15), חֲמָסִי, 'the wrong done to me' (Gn 16:5), לְדָרְשֵׁנִי, 'to consult me' (Je 37:7).

111 Possessive, e.g. בְּרִיתִי, 'my covenant' (Gn 6:18), מַלְכֵּנוּ, 'our king' (Ps 89:19).

112 After prepositions the suffixed forms of pronouns are used.

Demonstrative (Deictic)

113 זֶה is used when something is first mentioned or about to be mentioned; הוּא indicates something already referred to, e.g. וְהָיָה אֲשֶׁר אֹמַר אֵלֶיךָ זֶה יֵלֵךְ אִתָּךְ הוּא יֵלֵךְ אִתָּךְ, 'The one of whom I shall say to you, "This man shall go with you," he it is shall go with you' (Ju 7:4).

114 Explicative, as the subject of a non-verbal clause, e.g. זֶה הַיּוֹם, 'This is the day' (Ju 4:14), אֵלֶּה שְׁמוֹת בְּנֵי־עֵשָׂו, 'These are the names of Esau's sons' (Gn 36:10), הוּא יָם הַמֶּלַח, 'that is the Salt Sea' (Gn 14:3).

115 Anaphoric, when it functions as a copula, e.g. אֶרֶץ מִצְרַיִם לְפָנֶיךָ הוּא, 'The land of Egypt is before you' (Gn 47:6), י׳ הוּא הָאֱלֹהִים, 'Yahweh is the true God' (I Kg 18:39). Note that this form is used even with a first person, e.g. אֲנִי־הוּא הַמְדַבֵּר, 'It is I who am speaking' (Is 52:6), or a second person, e.g. אַתָּה־הוּא הָאֱלֹהִים, 'You are the true God' (II Sm 7:28).

116 Antithetical, when repeated to express a contrast, e.g. זֶה . . . זֶה, 'this . . . that,' 'the one . . . the other' (Is 6:3), אֵלֶּה . . . אֵלֶּה, 'some . . . others' (Jo 8:22).

117 Adjectival (cf. §74), either as an attributive adjective, e.g. הַדְּבָרִים הָאֵלֶּה, 'these words' (I Sm 18:23), or in apposition, e.g. דְּבָרֵנוּ זֶה, 'this matter of ours' (Jo 2:20).

23

118 Enclitic, employed as an undeclined particle for emphasis, e.g. מַה־זֶּה הָיָה, 'What in the world has happened?'
(I Sm 10:11), לָמָּה־זֶּה, 'why ever?' (I Sm 17:28), הִנֵּה־זֶה
מַלְאָךְ, 'All of a sudden there was an angel' (I Kg 19:5),
עַתָּה זֶה, 'now indeed' (I Kg 17:24), הַאַתָּה זֶה בְּנִי, 'Are
you *really* my son?' (Gn 27:21); cf. I Kg 18:7, 17, Nu
13:17. With the verb עָשָׂה the form זֹאת is always used,
e.g. מַה־זֹּאת עָשִׂית, 'What ever have you done?' (Gn 3:13);
cf. Gn 42:28. The unchangeable form זֶה regularly precedes in expressions such as זֶה עֶשְׂרִים שָׁנָה, 'for twenty
years now' (Gn 31:38); cf. Gn 27:36, 43:10.

Interrogative

119 The forms מִי and מָה are indeclinable.
The particle מִי has the following uses:

120 - Interrogative, 'who?', e.g. מִי הִגִּיד לָךְ, 'Who told you?'
(Gn 3:11); cf. Ju 18:3.

121 - Indefinite, 'whoever,' e.g. מִי לַיהוָה אֵלָי, 'Whoever is for
Yahweh (come) to me!' (Ex 32:26); cf. Ju 7:3.

122 - Desiderative or optative, to be rendered 'would that!',
'if only!', as in מִי־יְשִׂמֵנִי שֹׁפֵט בָּאָרֶץ, 'If only I might
be appointed judge in the land!' (II Sm 15:4). It is
usually expanded to מִי־יִתֵּן (cf. §547).

123 - Adverbial, 'how?', a barely possible use in מִי יָקוּם
יַעֲקֹב, 'How can Jacob stand?' (Am 7:2, 5).
The particle מָה has the following uses:

124 - Interrogative, 'what?', e.g. מֶה עָשִׂיתָ, 'What did you
do?' (Gn 4:10); cf. Gn 37:26.

125 - Indefinite, 'whatever,' is less common, e.g. וּדְבַר מַה־
יַּרְאֵנִי וְהִגַּדְתִּי לָךְ, 'Whatever matter he shows me, I will
tell you' (Nu 23:3); cf. I Sm 19:3, Ju 9:48.

126 - Adverbial, 'how?', e.g. מָה אֶתֵּן זֶה לִפְנֵי מֵאָה אִישׁ, 'How
can I set this before a hundred men?' (II Kg 4:43); cf.
Gn 44:16, Nu 23:8; or 'why?', e.g. מָה־אוֹחִיל לַיהוָה עוֹד,
'Why should I wait for Yahweh any longer?' (II Kg 6:33);
cf. II Kg 7:3, Ex 14:15, although this is usually לָמָּה.

24

127   - Exclamatory, 'how!', e.g. מַה־נּוֹרָא הַמָּקוֹם הַזֶּה, 'How awe-
some this place is!' (Gn 28:17); cf. Nu 24:5.

128   - Negative (cf. §428), a rare use arising from its em-
ployment in rhetorical questions, e.g. מַה־לָּנוּ חֵלֶק בְּדָוִד
וְלֹא־נַחֲלָה בְּבֶן־יִשַׁי, 'What portion have we in David? There
is no inheritance in Jesse's son' (I Kg 12:16; parallel
to אֵין in II Sm 20:1), וְאֶחְדְּלָה מַה־מִּנִּי יַהֲלֹךְ, 'If I am si-
lent, it will not leave me' (Jb 16:6, parallel to לֹא);
cf. Ca 8:4 (note the parallel with privative אִם in 2:7).

Relative

129 The true relative pronoun זֹ, found in Phoenician, e.g.
בת ז בני יחמלך, 'the house which Yehimilk built' (KAI,
4:1), is preserved in Hebrew solely as an archaism in
poetry, e.g. עַם־זוּ גָּאָלְתָּ, 'the people whom you redeemed'
(Ex 15:13); cf. Ex 15:16, Ps 9:16, 10:2. Variant forms
occur in וְעֵדֹתִי זוֹ אֲלַמְּדֵם, 'my statutes which I will teach
them' (Ps 132:12) and לִוְיָתָן זֶה־יָצַרְתָּ, 'Leviathan whom you
formed' (Ps 104:26); cf. Jb 19:19. In north Palestinian
and later Hebrew the form ־שֶׁ is also current (Ju 7:12,
II Kg 6:11, Ec 1:14; cf. §§470f.). Otherwise the relative is expressed by the particle אֲשֶׁר (cf. §§462f.) as
in Moabite.

Reflexive

130 Hebrew possesses no partitive, distributive, reciprocal
or reflexive pronouns. The last may be expressed by the
use of suffixed personal pronouns, e.g. הַאֹתִי הֵם מַכְעִסִים
. . ., הֲלוֹא אֹתָם, 'Is it me that they anger? . . . Is it
not themselves?' (Je 7:19), or by נֶפֶשׁ, 'person.' That
these are interchangeable is clear from a comparison of
נִשְׁבַּע אֲדֹנָי יְי בְּנַפְשׁוֹ, 'The Lord Yahweh has sworn by himself' (Am 6:8) with אֲשֶׁר נִשְׁבַּעְתָּ לָהֶם בָּךְ, 'those to whom
you swore by your own self' (Ex 32:13). The reflexive
may also be expressed by the Nip̄ᶜal or Hiṯpō̄ᶜel themes
(cf. §§135, 152, 154f.).

Distributive

131   To express the distributive 'each' Hebrew employs אִישׁ,
e.g. וַיַּחַלְמוּ חֲלוֹם שְׁנֵיהֶם אִישׁ חֲלֹמוֹ, 'they both had a dream,
each his own dream' (Gn 40:5); cf. Ex 12:3, Jb 42:11.

Reciprocal

132   The lack of reciprocal pronouns is compensated for by
the use of אִישׁ . . . אָחִיו (Dt 1:16), אִישׁ . . . רֵעֵהוּ (Gn
11:3, 7), or זֶה . . . זֶה (Is 6:3); cf. §116. Mutual action may also be expressed by the *Nip̄ʿal* or *Hiṯpāʿel*
themes (cf. §§137, 153), or the rare *Pōʿel* (cf. §156).

III Syntax of the Verb

1 THEME

Qal

133 Stative, expressing a state or condition, e.g. כָּבֵד, 'be
     heavy,' קָטֹן, 'be small,' בּוֹשׁ, 'be ashamed.'

134 Fientive, expressing an action (cf. pp. 4f.), e.g. הָלַךְ,
     'go,' נָתַן, 'give,' שִׂים, 'put.'

Nip̄ʿal

135 Reflexive, e.g. נִשְׁמַר, 'guard oneself,' נִסְתַּר, 'hide one-
     self,' נֶהְפַּךְ, 'turn oneself over' (Ru 3:8).

136 Middle, e.g. נִשְׁאַל, 'ask for oneself,' i.e. 'ask leave'
     (I Sm 20:6, 28), נִכְבַּד, 'achieve glory for oneself' (Ezk
     39:13).

137 Reciprocal, e.g. נִשְׁפַּט, 'go to law with one another' (I
     Sm 12:7), נִלְחַם, 'fight with one another,' נָצָה, 'struggle
     together.'

138 Tolerative, e.g. נִדְרַשׁ, 'let oneself be consulted' (Ezk
     14:3), נִזְהַר, 'let oneself be instructed/warned.'

139 Passive of the Qal, e.g. נוֹלַד, 'be born,' of the Piʿel,
     e.g. נִכְבַּד, 'be honoured,' or of the Hip̄ʿil, e.g. נִשְׁמַד,
     'be destroyed.'

Piʿel/Puʿal

140 As Goetze has demonstrated, the usual description of
     these themes as 'intensive' is inaccurate.

141 Factitive, with stative verbs, e.g. כִּבַּד, 'honour,' מִלֵּא,
     'fill,' חִדֵּשׁ, 'restore,' 'renew.'

142 Causative, with fientive verbs, e.g. לִמַּד, 'teach,' יִלֵּד,
     'help in childbirth.' This is not a common use.

143 Plurative or repetitive (perhaps having a separate ori-
     gin, with infixed assimilated *n*?), e.g. שִׁבֵּר, 'smash to

27

bits,' בִּקֵּשׁ, 'search,' הִלֵּךְ, 'walk about,' 'prowl,' קִבֵּר, 'bury large numbers,' שִׁאֵל, 'beg' (Ps 109:10).

144 Denominative, when verbs are derived from nouns, e.g. שֵׁרֵשׁ (<שֹׁרֶשׁ), 'root out,' 'uproot,' כִּהֵן (<כֹּהֵן), 'act as priest,' שִׁלֵּשׁ (<שָׁלוֹשׁ), 'do three times,' 'triple.'

145 Delocutive, with verbs derived from a locution, e.g. אִשֵּׁר (<אַשְׁרֵי), 'pronounce happy,' 'felicitate,' נִקָּה (<נָקִי), 'pronounce innocent,' צִדֵּק (<צַדִּיק), 'pronounce in the right.'

146 Privative, e.g. סִקֵּל, 'clear of stones' (Is 5:2 <סָקַל, 'cast stones'), חִטֵּא, 'purify from sin' (Ps 51:9 <חָטָא, 'commit sin').

Hip̄ʿīl/Hᵒp̄ʿal

147 Causative, e.g. הוֹצִיא, 'bring out,' הֶאֱכִיל, 'feed,' הֶרְאָה, 'show.'

148 Delocutive (cf. §145), e.g. הִצְדִּיק (<צַדִּיק), 'pronounce in the right,' 'justify,' הִרְשִׁיעַ (<רָשָׁע), 'pronounce in the wrong,' 'condemn,' הֵקַל, 'belittle.'

149 Factitive, although rare, is found with some stative verbs, e.g. הֶלְאָה, 'exhaust,' הֶעֱמִיק, 'deepen,' הִגְבִּיהַּ, 'make high,' הִקְרִיב, 'bring near,' הֶחֱיָה, 'make live,' 'revive.'

150 Intransitive, which indicates the entry into a state or condition and the remaining in the same, e.g. הִקְשָׁה, 'become difficult,' הִזְקִין, 'grow old,' הוֹבִישׁ, 'become dry,' הִמְתִּיק, 'become sweet'; also the exhibiting of a state or quality, e.g. הִשְׂכִּיל, 'act wisely,' הֶעֱרִים, 'act craftily,' הִרְשִׁיעַ, 'act wickedly.'

151 Denominative (rarer than *Piʿel*; cf. §144), e.g. הִשְׁרִישׁ, 'grow roots' (contrast שֵׁרֵשׁ, הִקְרִין, 'grow horns,' הִלְשִׁין, 'slander' (Pr 30:10), הֵימִין, 'go right.'

Hitpᵊʿel

152 Reflexive-iterative, e.g. הִתְחַבֵּא, 'hide oneself,' הִתְהַלֵּךְ, 'walk about' (cf. French *se promener*), הִתְקַדֵּשׁ, 'sanctify

28

oneself,' הִתְפַּלֵּל, 'intercede' (cf. German *sich verwenden*).
153 Reciprocal-iterative, e.g. הִתְרָאָה, 'look at one another.'
154 Reflexive-factitive, e.g. הִתְגַּדֵּל, 'aggrandize oneself.'
155 Reflexive-estimative, e.g. הִשְׂתָּרֵר, 'regard oneself as a
prince,' הִתְחַלָּה, 'feign illness,' הִתְנַבֵּא, 'play the part
of a prophet,' הִשְׁתַּכֵּר, 'play the drunkard.'

Pō‘el
156 Reciprocal, e.g. שׁוֹפֵט, 'be an opponent at law' (Jb 9:15).

2 VOICE

Active
157 Expressed by the *Qal*, *Pi‘el* and *Hip̄‘îl* themes.

Middle
158 Expressed by means of the *Nip̄‘al* theme (cf. §136).

Passive
159 Passive themes may be employed, viz. *Qal* passive יֻתַּן
(Nu 32:5; cf. יֻקַּח, etc.), *Nip̄‘al*, *Pu‘al*, *Hop̄‘al*.
160 Active themes in the impersonal third person singular
or plural may be used, e.g. קָרָא (Gn 11:9), יִתְּנוּ (I Kg
18:23).

3 ASPECT

Perfect
161 Stative, expressing a state or condition. This is normally rendered by a present tense in English, e.g. וַאֲנִי
זָקַנְתִּי וָשַׂבְתִּי, 'I am old and grey' (I Sm 12:2).
162 Completed action, expressing actions completed either
in reality or in the thought of the speaker. It may be
translated in English by: (1) a past tense, e.g. בָּרָא
אֱלֹהִים, 'God created' (Gn 1:1); (2) a perfect tense with
'have' denoting action completed in the past but con-
tinuing in its effects into the present, e.g. פֵּרַשְׂתִּי יָדַי
אֵלֶיךָ, 'I have stretched out my hands to you' (Ps 143:

29

6), שָׁכַח אֵל הִסְתִּיר פָּנָיו, 'God has forgotten; he has hidden his face' (Ps 10:11); cf. Is 1:4; (3) a pluperfect tense to indicate action anterior to the accompanying verb, e.g. רָחֵל גְּנָבָתַם, 'Rachel had stolen them' (Gn 31: 32); cf. I Sm 9:15, II Kg 7:17 (the subject usually precedes; cf. §573, 4); (4) a future perfect tense, e.g. אֲשֶׁר נָתַן־לָךְ, '(the land) which he will have given you' (Dt 8:10), אֲשֶׁר הִדַּחְתִּים שָׁם, '(all the places) to which I shall have driven them' (Je 8:3).

163 Experience, when a fientive verb expresses a state of mind, e.g. יָדַעְתִּי, 'I know' (Gn 4:9), מָאַסְתִּי, 'I despise' (Am 5:21), זָכַרְנוּ, 'We remember' (Nu 11:5).

164 Instantaneous action, expressing an act in the present which by that very act is completed, e.g. הַעִדֹתִי, 'I testify' (Dt 8:19), נִשְׁבַּעְתִּי, 'I swear' (Je 22:5), הֲרִימֹתִי, 'I lift up (my hand in an oath)' (Gn 14:22), אָמַרְתִּי, 'I say' (II Sm 19:30).

165 Certitude (the so-called 'prophetic perfect'), expressing a vivid future when the action is deemed 'as good as done,' as in the case of Greek ὄλωλα, e.g. הֵן גָּוַעְנוּ אָבַדְנוּ כֻּלָּנוּ אָבָדְנוּ, 'See, we have perished! We are done for, we are all done for!' (Nu 17:27); cf. Is 5:13.

166 Conditional. The perfect aspect is used in unreal conditions in the past, e.g. לוּ הַחֲיִתֶם אוֹתָם לֹא הָרַגְתִּי אֶתְכֶם, 'If you had let them live, I would not have killed you' (Ju 8:19); cf. Gn 43:10. It is also used in expressions of unfulfilled desire, e.g. לוּ־מַתְנוּ בְּאֶרֶץ מִצְרַיִם, 'If only we had died in the land of Egypt!' (Nu 14:2), with which contrast לוּ נָמוּת, 'If only we might die!' (cf. §174).

Imperfect

167 Incompleted action, either in the present, e.g. מַה־תְּבַקֵּשׁ, 'What are you looking for?' (Gn 37:15); cf. I Sm 1:8; or in the past, after טֶרֶם and בְּטֶרֶם, e.g. טֶרֶם יִשְׁכָּבוּ, 'before they lay down' (Gn 19:4) and עַד, e.g. וְעַד יִתְקַדְּשׁוּ הַכֹּהֲנִים, 'till the priests had sanctified themselves' (II

30

Ch 29:34. Note that this is not the preterite (§176).
It may also be used for simple futurity, regularly with
statives but also with fientives, e.g. וְהֵן לֹא־יַאֲמִינוּ לִי
וְלֹא יִשְׁמְעוּ בְּקֹלִי, 'See, they will not believe me nor listen to my voice' (Ex 4:1); cf. Ex 6:1. Sometimes this
may involve the future from a past point of view, e.g.
שָׁמְעוּ כִּי־שָׁם יֹאכְלוּ לָחֶם, 'They heard that they would have
a meal there' (Gn 43:25); cf. Gn 43:7.

168 Frequentative or habitual, indicating action repeated
either at any time, e.g. כָּכָה יַעֲשֶׂה אִיּוֹב כָּל־הַיָּמִים, 'Thus
Job would do always' (Jb 1:5), כֹּה־יִתֵּן שְׁלֹמֹה לְחִירָם שָׁנָה
בְשָׁנָה, 'Solomon would give this to Hiram year by year'
(I Kg 5:25), or customarily at a given time, e.g. כַּאֲשֶׁר
תַּעֲשֶׂינָה הַדְּבֹרִים, 'as bees do' (Dt 1:44), לֹא יוּכְלוּן הַמִּצְרִים,
'the Egyptians were not able' (Gn 43:32), מִכָּל־מַאֲכָל אֲשֶׁר
יֵאָכֵל, 'some of every kind of food that might be eaten'
(Gn 6:21). This is especially common in proverbial say-
ings, e.g. בֵּן חָכָם יְשַׂמַּח־אָב, 'A wise son makes a father
glad' (Pr 15:20; in parallelism with a participle).

169 Potential, expressing ability, but less emphatic than
יָכֹל with the infinitive, e.g. אֵיכָה אֶשָּׂא לְבַדִּי, 'How can I
bear by myself?' (Dt 1:12; cf. לֹא־אוּכַל לְבַדִּי שְׂאֵת אֶתְכֶם in
v. 9); cf. II Kg 9:37, Jb 4:17.

170 Permissive, expressing an idea to be rendered by 'may,'
e.g. מִכֹּל עֵץ הַגָּן אָכֹל תֹּאכֵל, 'You may certainly eat from
every tree of the garden' (Gn 2:16), אֶת־שְׁנֵי בָנַי תָּמִית אִם־
לֹא אֲבִיאֶנּוּ אֵלֶיךָ, 'You may slay my two sons if I do not
return him to you' (Gn 42:37), וְאַחַר דַּבְּרִי תַּלְעִיג, 'After
I have spoken, you may mock' (Jb 21:3).

171 Desiderative, expressing a wish, e.g. הֲתֵלְכִי עִם־הָאִישׁ הַזֶּה,
'Will you (i.e. do you wish to) go with this man?' (Gn
24:58), אִם־אֹתָהּ תִּקַּח־לְךָ קָח, 'If you want to take it, do
so' (I Sm 21:10); cf. Ju 4:8.

172 Obligative, to be translated by 'ought to,' e.g. מַעֲשִׂים
אֲשֶׁר לֹא־יֵעָשׂוּ עָשִׂיתָ עִמָּדִי, 'You have done things to me that

ought not to be done' (Gn 20:9); cf. Gn 34:7, Lv 4:13,
II Sm 13:12, I Kg 18:27.

173 Injunctive, expressing a strong command, to be rendered
by 'must,' 'shall,' 'are to,' etc., e.g. וְאֶת־חֻקֹּתַי תִּשְׁמְרוּ,
'You must keep my statutes' (Lv 18:4), עַל־גְּחֹנְךָ תֵלֵךְ וְעָפָר
תֹּאכַל, 'On your belly you shall go, and dust you shall
eat' (Gn 3:14); cf. Ex 21:12. With the negative particle
לֹא it expresses prohibition (which is stronger than the
vetitive; cf. §186), e.g. Ex 20:13-17.

174 Conditional. The imperfect aspect is used in real conditions in the future, e.g. אִם־אֶצְדָּק פִּי יַרְשִׁיעֵנִי, 'Though I
am in the right, my mouth will condemn me' (Jb 9:20),
כִּי־אֵלֵךְ בְּגֵיא צַלְמָוֶת, 'if I walk through a valley of deep
darkness' (Ps 23:4), or in wishes with לוּ, e.g. לוּ שָׁקוֹל
יִשָּׁקֵל כַּעְשִׂי, 'If only my vexation might be weighed out!'
(Jb 6:2; contrast §166).

175 The imperfect aspect is employed after telic particles,
viz. פֶּן (cf. §461), e.g. Gn 3:3; לְמַעַן (אֲשֶׁר) (cf. §367),
e.g. Gn 12:13, Je 42:6; לְבִלְתִּי (cf. §424), e.g. Ex 20:
20; בַּעֲבוּר (cf. §522), e.g. Gn 27:4; אֲשֶׁר (cf. §466), e.g.
Dt 4:40.

Preterite

176 This form may be distinguished from the imperfect by its
vocalization and accent in the *Qal* of weak verbs and the
Hipʿil of all verbs. It was originally a true past tense,
as in Ugaritic *whln.ʿnt.lbth.tmġyn / tštql.ʾilt.lhklh /
wl.šbʿt.tmtḫṣh.bʿmq*, 'See! Anat proceeded to her house,
the goddess made for her palace; but she was not sated
with her fighting in the valley' (UTB, ʿnt II.iii.17-19)
and in Moabite עמרי מלך ישראל ויענו את מאב ימן רבן כי
יאנף כמש בארצה, 'Omri, king of Israel, oppressed Moab
for a long time, for Chemosh was angry with his land'
(KAI, 181:4-6); cf. also Akkadian *iprus*.

177 In classical Hebrew this form is preserved in archaic
(poetic) language, e.g. תִּבְלָעֵמוֹ, 'it swallowed them,' pa-

32

rallel to נָטִיתָ (Ex 15:12; cf. 14f.), אִוָּלֵד, 'I was born'
(Jb 3:3; cf. 11); cf. Dt 32:10, Is 5:12, 9:17. It occurs
in prose after אָז, e.g. אָז יַקְהֵל שְׁלֹמֹה, 'at that time Solomon convoked' (I Kg 8:1), אָז יָשִׁיר־מֹשֶׁה, 'at that time
Moses sang' (Ex 15:1); cf. Dt 4:41, Nu 21:17, Jo 8:30,
10:12 (note that the perfect aspect is found in Gn 4:26,
Jo 10:33, II Kg 14:8). This is the form which occurs with
the *waw*-'consecutive' (cf. §178), from which use, by
analogy, came the construction *waw*-'consecutive' with
the perfect (cf. §179).

Consecution

178   With 'consecutive' *waw* expressing temporal sequence (cf.
§496) or result (cf. §525):
- 'Consecutive' *waw* with the 'imperfect,' originally the
preterite with the early pronunciation of the conjunction archaistically retained as *wa-*, now equivalent to
the perfect aspect in initial position in a clause, e.g.
וְהַמַּיִם גָּבְרוּ מְאֹד מְאֹד עַל־הָאָרֶץ וַיְכֻסּוּ כָּל־הֶהָרִים, 'The waters
having increased very considerably on the earth, all
the mountains were covered' (Gn 7:19); cf. Gn 18:7, I
Sm 15:20.

179   - By analogy, *waw* occurs with the perfect. Since it was
a later development, the conjunction suffered the normal later vowel reduction, becoming $w^ə$. This is equivalent to the imperfect aspect in initial position in a
clause, e.g. פֶּן־יֶחְדַּל אָבִי מִן־הָאֲתֹנוֹת וְדָאַג לָנוּ, 'lest my
father cease concern for the asses and be anxious for
us' (I Sm 9:5); cf. Gn 18:18, 24:4.

180   With 'simple' *waw*:
- Occasionally this occurs with the imperfect aspect as
a simple imperfect, e.g. וַאֲפִיצֵם, 'I will scatter them'
(Gn 49:7); cf. Is 5:29. This seems to be confined mainly
to poetry (exceptions are I Kg 18:27 and Dt 13:12).

181   - 'Simple' *waw* with the precative expresses purpose (cf.
§§187, 518), e.g. וְאֶעֱשֶׂה עִמּוֹ חֶסֶד, 'that I may show kind-

33

ness to him' (II Sm 9:1), or occasionally a command (cf.
§185), e.g. וִיהִי־נָא פִּי־שְׁנַיִם בְּרוּחֲךָ אֵלָי, 'Do let a double
portion of your spirit come to me' (II Kg 2:9).

182 - 'Simple' *waw* with the perfect may occur in biblical
Hebrew when two or more verbs are in a closely related
series, e.g. הוּא הֵסִיר אֶת־הַבָּמוֹת וְשִׁבַּר אֶת־הַמַּצֵּבֹת וְכָרַת אֶת־
הָאֲשֵׁרָה וְכִתַּת נְחַשׁ הַנְּחֹשֶׁת, 'He it was who removed the high
places, smashed the pillars, cut down the sacred pole
and beat the bronze snake to pieces' (II Kg 18:4); cf.
II Kg 21:6, 23:4f., II Sm 7:9-13. A clear exception is
וְהִרְאַנִי י׳, 'Yahweh showed me' (II Kg 8:10); examples
such as וְנָעַל (II Sm 13:18) and וְהִכָּה (I Kg 20:21), should
perhaps be vocalized as absolute infinitives (cf. §210).
In late usage the *waw*-'consecutive' construction breaks
down, as in וְנָתַתִּי אֶת־לִבִּי לִדְרוֹשׁ וְלָתוּר בַּחָכְמָה, 'I set my
mind to inquire and investigate by means of wisdom' (Ec
1:13); cf. Ec 2:12f.

4 MOOD

Precative

183 This is identical in form, though not in origin, with
the preterite.

184 Optative, expressing a strong desire or wish (cf. §546),
e.g. יְחִי הַמֶּלֶךְ, 'May the king live!' (I Sm 10:24), יָקֶם
אֶת־דְּבָרוֹ י׳, 'May Yahweh confirm his word!' (I Sm 1:23),
אֹכְלָה בָשָׂר, 'I would eat meat!' (Dt 12:20); cf. Dt 17:14.
For negation אַל is used, e.g. אַל־אֶרְאֶה בְּמוֹת הַיֶּלֶד, 'May
I not witness the lad's death!' (Gn 21:16); cf. Je 17:18.

185 Jussive and cohortative, expressing a command in the
third and first persons respectively (lacking in the
imperative), e.g. נֵלְכָה וְנַעַבְדָה אֱלֹהִים אֲחֵרִים, 'Let us go
and serve other gods!' (Dt 13:7); cf. Ju 15:2. Sometimes these occur after 'simple' *waw* when purpose is not
intended (cf. §181), e.g. וְיִתְּנוּ־לָנוּ שְׁנַיִם פָּרִים וְיִבְחֲרוּ
לָהֶם הַפָּר הָאֶחָד וִינַתְּחֻהוּ וְיָשִׂימוּ עַל־הָעֵצִים, 'Let two bulls be

34

given to us; let them choose one bull for themselves, cut it up and put it on the wood' (I Kg 18:23); cf. II Kg 2:9.

186 Vetitive, the negative of the imperative (cf. §188), is expressed by אַל with the second person of the precative, e.g. זְכֹר אַל־תִּשְׁכַּח, 'Remember; do not forget' (Dt 9:7); cf. I Kg 13:22.

187 Purpose, employed after 'simple' *waw* in telic clauses (cf. §§518, 181), e.g. וְהָבִיאָה לִּי וְאֹכֵלָה, 'Bring it to me that I may eat' (Gn 27:4); cf. I Kg 21:2.

Imperative

188 Command, in the second person only; otherwise the precative must be used (cf. §185) just as in the case of the vetitive (cf. §186).

189 Purpose may occasionally be intended when an imperative follows *waw* (cf. §519), e.g. לְכִי אִיעָצֵךְ נָא עֵצָה וּמַלְּטִי אֶת־נַפְשֵׁךְ, 'Come, just let me counsel you, that you may save your life' (I Kg 1:12); cf. II Kg 5:10, II Sm 21:3.

190 A conditional meaning may also be expressed by two imperatives joined by *waw*, e.g. זֹאת עֲשׂוּ וִחְיוּ, 'If you do this, you will live' (Gn 42:18); cf. Is 36:16.

191 An imperative may serve as an interjection when used in the singular as a particle, e.g. קוּם (Ex 32:1), הָבָה (Gn 11:3, 7), לְכָה (Gn 19:32).

5 VERBAL NOUNS

Construct Infinitive

192 As subject of a sentence, e.g. לֹא־טוֹב הֱיוֹת הָאָדָם לְבַדּוֹ, 'It is not good for the man to be alone' (Gn 2:18); cf. I Sm 18:23. It may also be introduced by the preposition לְ (cf. §276), e.g. וְאִם רַע בְּעֵינֵיכֶם לַעֲבֹד אֶת־יְ, 'If it displeases you to serve Yahweh' (Jo 24:15).

193 As object of a verb, e.g. לֹא אֵדַע צֵאת וָבֹא, 'I do not know how to go in or out' (I Kg 3:7); cf. Dt 10:10; also with

35

the introducing לְ (cf. §276), e.g. לֹא־נְתַתִּיךָ לִנְגֹּעַ אֵלֶיהָ, 'I did not allow you to touch her' (Gn 20:6). This may even occur with the accusative particle, e.g. וְאֵת יָדַעְתִּי הִתְרַגֶּזְךָ אֵלָי, 'I know your frenzied raging at me' (II Kg 19:27 = Is 37:28).

194 As a genitive, e.g. בְּיוֹם אֲכָלְךָ מִמֶּנּוּ, 'on the day that you eat from it' (Gn 2:17); cf. Gn 29:7. So always after prepositions (cf. §36).

195 Equivalent to a gerund, with לְ of norm (cf. §274), to be translated 'by . . .-ing,' e.g. וְשָׁמְרוּ בְנֵי־יִשְׂרָאֵל אֶת־הַשַּׁבָּת לַעֲשׂוֹת אֶת־הַשַּׁבָּת לְדֹרֹתָם בְּרִית עוֹלָם, 'The Israelites are to keep the sabbath by observing the sabbath throughout their generations as an eternal covenant' (Ex 31:16); cf. I Sm 14:33, 12:17; so לֵאמֹר, 'by saying,' i.e. 'by virtue of the statement' (Ex 5:19). The negative uses לְבִלְתִּי (cf. §423), e.g. הִשָּׁמֶר לְךָ פֶּן־תִּשְׁכַּח אֶת־יְ/ אֱלֹהֶיךָ לְבִלְתִּי שְׁמֹר מִצְוֹתָיו, 'Take care lest you forget Yahweh your God by not keeping his commandments' (Dt 8:11). The meaning is similar to Latin *(ad) portandi/um/ō* (especially in the ablative).

196 Equivalent to a gerundive, with לְ of product (cf. §278), best translated 'is to be . . .-ed,' e.g. מֶה לַעֲשׂוֹת לָךְ, 'What is to be done for you?' (II Kg 4:13); cf. Gn 15:12, Jo 2:5, Es 3:14. The negative is formed with לֹא (cf. §397), e.g. לֹא לְהַזְכִּיר בְּשֵׁם יְ/, 'The name of Yahweh is not to be mentioned' (Am 6:10), or, in late usage, by אֵין (cf. §410), e.g. וַיָּבוֹא עַד לִפְנֵי שַׁעַר־הַמֶּלֶךְ כִּי אֵין לָבוֹא אֶל־שַׁעַר הַמֶּלֶךְ בִּלְבוּשׁ שָׂק, 'He came near the king's gate, for the king's gate was not to be entered in clothing of sackcloth' (Es 4:2). This is similar in meaning to Latin *portandus est*, 'it is to be carried.'

197 Purpose, with לְ (cf. §277), לְמַעַן (cf. §367), or בַּעֲבוּר (cf. §522), and in the negative with לְבִלְתִּי (cf. §424).

198 Consequence or result, with לְ (cf. §279), may be translated 'thus . . .-ing,' e.g. לְהַכְעִיסוֹ, 'thus provoking

36

him to anger' (Dt 4:25); cf. Nu 11:11, Lv 20:3, I Kg 2: 27. It may also be translated 'so as to . . .,' or the like, e.g. מַדּוּעַ מָצָאתִי חֵן בְּעֵינֶיךָ לְהַכִּירֵנִי, 'Why have I found favour in your sight so that notice is taken of me?' (Ru 2:10). Less often לְמַעַן is used (cf. §368), e.g. לְמַעַן חַלֵּל אֶת־שֵׁם קָדְשִׁי, 'thus profaning my holy name' (Am 2:7); cf. II Kg 22:17).

199 Degree, with לְ (cf. §275), may be rendered as 'enough to . . .,' e.g. וַיֵּצֶר לְאַמְנוֹן לְהִתְחַלּוֹת בַּעֲבוּר תָּמָר אֲחֹתוֹ, 'Amnon was distressed enough to feign illness because of his sister Tamar' (II Sm 13:2); cf. Dt 9:20, II Kg 20:1.

200 Used frequently after prepositions, especially with temporal (cf. §§503-508), causal (cf. §535), or concessive (cf. §§531f.) meaning.

Absolute Infinitive

201 Of different origin from the construct infinitive, it normally take neither prefixes nor suffixes (but note §207).

202 As subject of a sentence it is restricted to poetry, e.g. הַכֵּר־פָּנִים בְּמִשְׁפָּט בַּל־טוֹב, 'To be partial in judgment is not good' (Pr 24:23); cf. Jb 6:25.

203 As object of a verb, usually in poetry, e.g. לֹא־יִתְּנֵנִי הָשֵׁב רוּחִי, 'He will not allow me to draw my breath' (Jb 9: 18); cf. Dt 28:56, Is 1:17.

204 In the adverbial accusative of manner (cf. §60), e.g. רִדְפוּ מַהֵר, 'Pursue quickly' (Jo 2:5), וְשָׁאַלְתָּ הֵיטֵב, 'You shall inquire diligently' (Dt 13:15), וַיִּגַּשׁ הַפְּלִשְׁתִּי הַשְׁכֵּם וְהַעֲרֵב, 'The Philistine approached early and late' (I Sm 17:16), וַתֵּשֶׁב לָהּ מִנֶּגֶד הַרְחֵק, 'She seated herself opposite at a distance' (Gn 21:16), הָחֵל וְכַלֵּה, 'from beginning to end' (I Sm 3:12).

205 To indicate emphasis, the absolute infinitive precedes the finite form of the same root (but not necessarily

37

the same theme), e.g. מוֹת תָּמוּת, 'You will surely die'
(Gn 2:17), טָרֹף טֹרַף, 'He has been torn to pieces' (Gn
44:28); cf. Am 9:8, Jb 6:2, Ex 21:12. Instances of this
construction in Ugaritic reveal that the infinitive was
in the nominative case, e.g. hm.ġmủ.ġmỉt, 'If you are
indeed thirsty' (UTB, 51.iv.34); so with a following infinitive: yspỉ.spủ, 'They will certainly eat' (UTB, 121.
ii.10). In Hebrew the infinitive may occasionally follow, e.g. יֵצֵא יָצוֹא, 'He would surely come out' (II Kg
5:11); so always with an imperative, e.g. הָרְגֵנִי נָא הָרֹג,
'Just kill me outright' (Nu 11:15). This infinitive normally precedes a negative. e.g. וְהוֹרֵשׁ לֹא הוֹרִישׁוֹ, 'They
did not drive them out completely' (Ju 1:28), וְהָמֵת אַל־
תְּמִיתֻהוּ, 'Do not put it to death at all' (I Kg 3:26); cf.
Ju 15:13, Is 30:19. It may, however, follow, as in לֹא
הַשְׁמֵיד אַשְׁמִיד, 'I will not utterly destroy' (Am 9:8); cf.
Ps 49:8, Gn 3:4.

206 To express continuous action or repetition it follows
the finite verb and is frequently of the same root, e.g.
וַיֹּאכַל גַּם־אָכוֹל אֶת־כַּסְפֵּנוּ, 'He has used up our money completely' (Gn 31:15); cf. Nu 11:32. This is quite common
with a second infinitive, e.g. הָלְכוּ הָלֹךְ וְגָעוֹ, 'They proceeded, lowing as they went' (I Sm 6:12); cf. Ju 14:9,
Gn 8:3, 5; also with an adjective, e.g. וַיֵּלֶךְ הָלוֹךְ וְרָב,
'It went on increasing' (I Sm 14:19), or a participle,
e.g. וַיֵּלֶךְ הָלוֹךְ וְקָרֵב, 'He came ever nearer' (II Sm 18:25).

207 As a genitive (rare), e.g. מִדֶּרֶךְ הַשְׂכֵּל, 'from the way of
understanding' (Pr 21:16); cf. Is 14:23. So also exceptionally after prepositions: לְהֵרָאֹה, 'to appear' (Ju 13:
21, I Sm 3:21), עַד־כַּלֵּה, 'until annihilating' (II Kg 13:
17, 19), וְאַחֲרֵי שָׁתֹה, 'after drinking' (I Sm 1:9).

208 As a substitute for a finite verb (cf. French voir, and
the Greek infinitive of command):

209 - For an imperfect, e.g. רָגוֹם אֹתוֹ בָאֲבָנִים כָּל־הָעֵדָה, 'All
the congregation shall stone him' (Nu 15:35); cf. Nu 30:

38

3, Dt 15:2, II Kg 4:43, Gn 17:10, Ex 12:48.

210   - For a perfect, e.g. וְנָפוֹץ הַכַּדִּים אֲשֶׁר בְּיָדָם, 'They shat-
tered the jars which were in their hands' (Ju 7:19); cf.
I Sm 2:28, Gn 41:43, Es 3:13, Ps 17:5. Thus the absolute infinitive sometimes precedes an independent personal pronoun, as often in Phoenician, e.g. קרא אנך, 'I
called' (KAI, 10:2); cf. KAI, 26A 1:6, 11. Hebrew examples are וְשַׁבֵּחַ אֲנִי, 'I lauded' (Ec 4:2), וְנַהֲפוֹךְ הוּא, 'but
it had been changed' (Es 9:1).

211   - For an imperative, e.g. הָלוֹךְ וְרָחַצְתָּ, 'Go and wash' (II
Kg 5:10); cf. Is 14:31 (parallel to an imperative).

212   - For a precative, e.g. (with modal אַל in the parallel
stich) פָּגוֹשׁ דֹּב שַׁכּוּל בְּאִישׁ וְאַל־כְּסִיל בְּאִוַּלְתּוֹ, 'Let a bear
bereft of her cubs encounter a man, and not a fool in
his folly' (Pr 17:12); cf. Lv 6:7.

Participle

213   To express continuous action, either in present time,
e.g. אֶת־אַחַי אָנֹכִי מְבַקֵּשׁ, 'It is my brothers for whom I am
looking' (Gn 37:16); cf. Gn 3:5, I Sm 23:1, II Kg 7:9;
or in past time, e.g. רַק בַּבָּמוֹת הוּא מְזַבֵּחַ וּמַקְטִיר, 'Nevertheless, it was on the high places that he was sacrificing and burning incense' (I Kg 3:3); cf. Jb 1:14. The
verb הָיָה may accompany the participle in such expressions of duration, e.g. וְהַנַּעַר הָיָה מְשָׁרֵת אֶת־י/, 'while the
lad was ministering to Yahweh' (I Sm 2:11); cf. Ju 16:
21, II Kg 17:25.

214   To indicate imminent action, e.g. וַאֲנִי הִנְנִי מֵבִיא אֶת־
הַמַּבּוּל מַיִם, 'As for me, I am about to bring the flood
waters' (Gn 6:17); cf. Gn 20:3, I Kg 20:13.

215   Adjectival, either attributive (cf. §73), e.g. אֵשׁ אֹכְלָה,
'a devouring fire' (Dt 4:24), or predicative (cf. §75),
e.g. וַיִּרְאוּ הַשֹּׁמְרִים אִישׁ יוֹצֵא, 'The Samaritans saw a man
going out' (Ju 1:24).

216   With a gerundive or admissive sense, meaning 'may be
. . .,' 'is to be . . .' This is normally the Nip̄ʿal

39

theme, e.g. נִכְבָּד, 'honourable,' נוֹרָא, 'terrible,' נֶחְמָד, 'desirable,' נֶאֱמָן, 'dependable,' נִתְעָב, 'detestable,' but the *Puʿal* may also be employed, e.g. מְהֻלָּל, 'laudable,' 'praiseworthy.'

217 Substantival, e.g. אֹיֵב, 'enemy,' רֹעֶה, 'shepherd,' חֹזֶה, 'seer,' שֹׁמֵר, 'watchman, spy.'

218 As equivalent to a relative clause, with the article (cf. §90), e.g. הַנִּרְאֶה אֵלָיו /י, 'Yahweh who had appeared to him' (Gn 12:7); cf. Gn 26:11, Ju 6:28.

219 In circumstantial clauses (cf. §494), e.g. וְאֵינְךָ אֹכֵל לֶחֶם, 'since you are eating no food' (I Kg 21:5), וְלוֹט יֹשֵׁב בְּשַׁעַר־סְדֹם, 'as Lot was sitting in the gate of Sodom' (Gn 19:1).

220 To express simultaneous action (synchronism); cf. §§236 f.), e.g. וֶאֱלִישָׁע רֹאֶה וְהוּא מְצַעֵק, 'As Elisha looked, he cried out' (II Kg 2:12); cf. II Kg 4:5, I Sm 25:20.

221 To indicate repetition or continuous action (similar to the absolute infinitive; cf. §206), e.g. וְדָוִד עֹלֶה בְמַעֲלֵה הַזֵּיתִים עֹלֶה וּבוֹכֶה, 'as David was climbing the slope of the Mount of Olives, weeping as he went' (II Sm 15:30); cf. I Sm 17:41, Ex 19:19.

222 To express an indefinite subject, e.g. כִּי־יִפֹּל הַנֹּפֵל מִמֶּנּוּ, 'if someone should fall from it' (Dt 22:8); cf. II Sm 17:9, Am 9:1, Je 9:23.

6 VERBAL CO-ORDINATION

223 In this construction, the second verb usually expresses the principal idea, while the first indicates the man-ner, and may conveniently be rendered in translation by the use of an adverb.

Two Finite Verbs

224 With the conjunction *waw*, e.g. וַיָּשָׁב וַיִּשְׁכָּב, 'He lay down again' (I Kg 19:6), וַיַּשְׁכֵּם יְהוֹשֻׁעַ בַּבֹּקֶר וַיִּפְקֹד אֶת־הָעָם, 'Jo-shua mustered the people first thing in the morning'

(Jo 8:10); cf. Gn 25:1, 24:18, Jo 8:14.

225 Asyndetic (usually confined to poetry), e.g. לֹא אוֹסִיף
עוֹד אֲרַחֵם, 'I will never again be merciful' (Ho 1:6); cf.
I Sm 2:3, Ps 106:13, Zp 3:7; for a prose example cf. Gn
30:31. But imperatives may be asyndetic even in prose,
e.g. שׁוּב שְׁכָב, 'Lie down again' (I Sm 3:5f.).

Finite Verb with Infinitive

226 The infinitive is usually introduced by לְ (cf. §276),
e.g. לָמָּה נַחְבֵּאתָ לִבְרֹחַ, 'Why did you run away furtively?'
(Gn 31:27), הִקְשִׁיתָ לִשְׁאוֹל, 'You have made a difficult request' (II Kg 2:10); cf. I Sm 15:12, Ps 126:2f.; however, the preposition may be omitted, e.g. מַדּוּעַ מִהַרְתֶּן
בֹּא הַיּוֹם, 'Why have you come so quickly today?' (Ex 2:
18); cf. Nu 22:15, I Sm 3:6, 8.

7 CONCORD OF SUBJECT AND VERB

227 When the subject precedes, the verb normally exhibits
concord of gender and number, e.g. וְתַרְדֵּמָה נָפְלָה עַל־אַבְרָם,
'Abram having fallen into a trance,' lit. 'a trance had
fallen upon Abram' (Gn 15:12), but note מַצּוֹת יֵאָכֵל, 'Unleavened loaves shall be eaten' (Ex 13:7).

228 When the verb precedes, the third masculine singular of
the verb is often used regardless of the gender or number of the subject, especially when the latter is inanimate or animal, e.g. יְהִי מְאֹרֹת בִּרְקִיעַ הַשָּׁמַיִם . . . וְהָיוּ
לְאֹתֹת, 'Let there be lights in the vault of the sky . . .
and let them become signs' (Gn 1:14); cf. Gn 39:5, II
Kg 3:18, 26; note that the following verbs exhibit concord. An example with a human subject is וַיֹּאמְרוּ שָׂרֵי סֻכּוֹת,
'The officials of Succoth said' (Ju 8:6).

229 Collectives often take the plural of the verb *ad sensum*,
e.g. וַיָּנֻסוּ אֲרָם, 'The Aramaeans fled' (I Kg 20:20); cf.
I Kg 18:24, Jb 1:14, I Sm 17:46.

230 Compound subjects usually take the verb in the singular

when the latter precedes, and in the plural when it follows, e.g. נַעַן רָחֵל וְלֵאָה וַתֹּאמַרְנָה לּוֹ, 'Rachel and Leah
said to him in reply' (Gn 31:14); cf. Nu 12:1f., I Sm
19:18, II Kg 3:9.

231 Dual subjects normally have the verb in the plural, e.g.
     תֶּחֱזַקְנָה יָדֶיךָ, 'Your hands will be strong' (Ju 7:11).

232 Subjects in the plural of respect (cf. §8) take the verb
     normally in the singular, e.g. אִם־אֲדֹנָיו יִתֶּן־לוֹ אִשָּׁה, 'if
     his master gives him a wife' (Ex 21:4); cf. Ex 21:29.

233 Abstract plural subjects (cf. §7) may have the verb in
     the singular, e.g. תִּתְחַדֵּשׁ כַּנֶּשֶׁר נְעוּרָיְכִי, 'Your youth will
     be renewed like an eagle's' (Ps 103:5).

234 Second feminine plural forms of verbs are rare, and are
     usually replaced by the masculine, e.g. כַּאֲשֶׁר עֲשִׂיתֶם, 'as
     you (i.e. Ruth's daughters-in-law) have done' (Ru 1:8);
     cf. Am 4:1, Jl 2:22. Similarly the masculine is used for
     the third feminine plural imperfect, e.g. וְשֶׁבַע הַשִּׁבֳּלִים
     הָרֵקוֹת . . . יִהְיוּ שֶׁבַע שְׁנֵי רָעָב, 'while the seven empty
     ears . . . will be seven years of famine' (Gn 41:27),
     especially when the verb precedes, e.g. אִם־יֵצְאוּ בְנוֹת־
     שִׁילוֹ, 'if the girls of Shiloh come out' (Ju 21:21); cf.
     I Kg 11:3, II Sm 4:1.

8 SYNCHRONISM (SIMULTANEOUS ACTION)

235 Indicated by two perfects with the subjects preceding,
     the first subject being asyndetic, e.g. הֵמָּה בָּאוּ בְּאֶרֶץ
     צוּף וְשָׁאוּל אָמַר לְנַעֲרוֹ, 'Just as they were coming into the
     land of Zuph, Saul said to his servant' (I Sm 9:5); cf.
     Gn 44:3f., Ju 15:14. This may even be accompanied by a
     negative, e.g. יְשַׁעְיָהוּ לֹא יָצָא הָעִיר הַתִּיכֹנָה וּדְבַר־יְ/ הָיָה
     אֵלָיו, 'No sooner had Isaiah gone forth from the central
     court than the word of Yahweh came to him' (II Kg 20:4).

236 Indicated by two participles, with subjects preceding,
     the first asyndetic (cf. §220; but note II Kg 2:12 with
     introductory waw!), e.g. הֵמָּה בָּאִים בְּתוֹךְ הָעִיר וְהִנֵּה שְׁמוּאֵל

הֵמָּה בָּאוּ בְּתוֹךְ הָעִיר וְהִנֵּה שְׁמוּאֵל יֹצֵא לִקְרָאתָם, 'Just as they were entering the city, there was Samuel coming out towards them' (I Sm 9:14); cf. II Kg 8:5, I Sm 25:20.

237 Indicated by a participle and a perfect, with subjects preceding, the first asyndetic, e.g. הֵמָּה עֹלִים בְּמַעֲלֵה הָעִיר וְהֵמָּה מָצְאוּ נְעָרוֹת, 'As they were climbing the slope to the city, they encountered some young women' (I Sm 9: 11); cf. I Sm 9:27.

IV Syntax of Particles

1 PREPOSITIONS

238 When a preposition governs more than one object, it is normal to repeat it before each one, e.g. לֶךְ־לְךָ מֵאַרְצְךָ וּמִמּוֹלַדְתְּךָ וּמִבֵּית אָבִיךָ, 'Go off from your native land and your paternal home' (Gn 12:1); cf. Ho 2:21. This is not, however, always the case, e.g. הַחֵפֶץ לַי׳ בְּעֹלוֹת וּזְבָחִים, 'Has Yahweh any pleasure in burnt offerings and sacrifices?' (I Sm 15:22).

The Preposition בְּ

239 Expresses rest or movement in place or time.

240 Locative, e.g. בַּבַּיִת, 'in the house,' בָּאָרֶץ, 'in/through the land,' בָּהָר, 'on the mountain.'

241 Temporal, expressing point of time, e.g. בַּבֹּקֶר, 'in the morning' (with which contrast the temporal accusative, §56). It may also be used with an infinitive (cf. §504), e.g. בְּהִבָּרְאָם, 'when they were created' (Gn 2:4), or with a noun clause (cf. §499), e.g. בְּעוֹד שְׁלֹשָׁה חֳדָשִׁים לַקָּצִיר, 'when there were still three months until the harvest' (Am 4:7).

242 Adversative, expressing disadvantage, e.g. יָדוֹ בַכֹּל וְיַד כֹּל בּוֹ, 'his hand against everyone and everyone's hand against him' (Gn 16:12); cf. I Sm 18:17. Sometimes this is to be rendered 'in spite of,' e.g. וְעַד־אָנָה לֹא־יַאֲמִינוּ בִי בְּכֹל הָאֹתוֹת אֲשֶׁר עָשִׂיתִי בְּקִרְבּוֹ, 'How long will they disbelieve me in spite of all the signs which I have performed among them?' (Nu 14:11); cf. Is 9:11.

243 Means or instrument, e.g. פֶּן־יִפְגָּעֵנוּ בַּדֶּבֶר אוֹ בֶחָרֶב, 'lest he attack us with pestilence or sword' (Ex 5:3); cf. Ex 16:3, Mi 4:14.

244 Transitivity, in the completion of some verbs where the

preposition really expresses means, but an accusative is normal, e.g. וְאַנִיעָה עֲלֵיכֶם בְּמוֹ רֹאשִׁי, 'I could shake my head at you' (Jb 16:4; contrast Ps 22:8), פָּעֲרוּ עָלַי בְּפִיהֶם, 'They have opened their mouths wide (i.e. gaped) at me' (Jb 16:10; contrast Jb 29:23); cf. Pr 6:13 (contrast Pr 10:10), Ps 46:7, Ex 7:20.

245 Agent (rare, usually expressed by לְ, cf. §280), e.g. שֹׁפֵךְ דַּם הָאָדָם בָּאָדָם דָּמוֹ יִשָּׁפֵךְ, 'He who sheds man's blood, by man shall his blood be shed' (Gn 9:6); cf. Nu 36:2.

246 Price or exchange, e.g. תְּנָה־לִּי אֶת־כַּרְמְךָ בְּכֶסֶף, 'Give me your vineyard in exchange for silver' (I Kg 21:6); cf. I Kg 10:29. Sometimes this is to be rendered 'at the risk/peril of,' e.g. <אֶשְׁתֶּה> הֲדַם הָאֲנָשִׁים הַהֹלְכִים בְּנַפְשׁוֹתָם, '<Can I drink> the blood of the men who went at the risk of their lives?' (II Sm 23:17); cf. I Kg 2:23.

247 Causal, e.g. הֲתַשְׁחִית בַּחֲמִשָּׁה אֶת־כָּל־הָעִיר, 'Will you destroy the whole city because of five?' (Gn 18:28); so with an infinitive (cf. §535), e.g. בְּעָזְבְכֶם אֶת־מִצְוֹת יי, 'because you have forsaken the commandments of Yahweh' (I Kg 18: 18) or a noun clause (cf. §534), e.g. בַּאֲשֶׁר אַתְּ־אִשְׁתּוֹ, 'because you are his wife' (Gn 39:9); cf. Gn 39:23.

248 Accompaniment, e.g. וַתָּבֹא יְרוּשָׁלְַמָה בְּחַיִל כָּבֵד מְאֹד, 'She entered Jerusalem with a very substantial retinue' (I Kg 10:2); cf. Gn 9:4, I Kg 19:19, Ex 10:9.

249 Identity (*essentiae*), with a predicate, explicative of some noun in the clause (cf. French *agir en témoin*, 'to act as witness,' *déguisé en pèlerin*, 'disguised as a pilgrim'), e.g. כִּי־אֱלֹהֵי אָבִי בְּעֶזְרִי, 'for the God of my father was my help' (Ex 18:4), בִּמְתֵי מְעָט, 'being but a few men' (Dt 26:5, 28:62); cf. Ex 6:3.

250 Specification, indicating the parts of which the whole consists, e.g. וַיִּגְוַע כָּל־בָּשָׂר הָרֹמֵשׂ עַל־הָאָרֶץ בָּעוֹף וּבַבְּהֵמָה וּבַחַיָּה וּבְכָל־הַשֶּׁרֶץ, 'All flesh that moved on earth expired: birds, cattle, wild beasts and all reptiles' (Gn 7:21); cf. Ex 12:19, 13:2.

45

251 Partitive, e.g. וְנָשְׂאוּ אִתְּךָ בְּמַשָּׂא הָעָם, 'And they will bear some of the burden of the people with you' (Nu 11:17); cf. II Kg 17:25.

252 Norm, expressing a state or condition, e.g. בְּשָׁלוֹם, 'in peace' (Gn 15:15), בְּתֻמּוֹ, 'in his integrity' (Pr 19:1), בְּצֶדֶק, 'in righteousness' (Lv 19:15), בְּרָעָה, 'with evil intent' (Ex 32:12).

253 Pregnant, with verbs of motion, expressing movement *to* resulting in rest *in* a place, e.g. וְשִׁלַּח אֶת־הַשָּׂעִיר בַּמִּדְבָּר, 'He shall send the goat forth into the wilderness' (Lv 16:22); cf. I Kg 11:2, Gn 19:8.

254 Distributive (cf. §102), e.g. יוֹם בְּיוֹם, 'day by day' (II Ch 30:21), שָׁנָה בְשָׁנָה, 'year after year' (I Sm 1:7); cf. Ne 8:18, I Sm 18:10, Ez 3:4, I Ch 27:1.

The Preposition כְּ

255 Expresses likeness, which may be either similarity or identity.

256 Comparative, e.g. הֲנִהְיָה כַּדָּבָר הַגָּדוֹל הַזֶּה, 'Has so great a thing as this happened?' (Dt 4:32); with an infinitive, וַיְשַׁסְּעֵהוּ כְּשַׁסַּע הַגְּדִי, 'He tore it to pieces as a kid is torn to pieces' (Ju 14:6); cf. II Sm 3:34. When used in a hypothetical sense this must be rendered 'as if,' 'as it were,' e.g. כְּהָנִיף שֵׁבֶט אֶת־מְרִימָיו כְּהָרִים מַטֶּה לֹא־עֵץ, 'as if a rod should brandish him who lifts it, as if a staff should lift what is not wood' (Is 10:15). It may also be used with a clause introduced by אֲשֶׁר, e.g. וְאֶתְּנָה כַּאֲשֶׁר תֹּאמְרוּ אֵלָי, 'that I may give according as you say to me' (Gn 34:12). The meaning 'such . . . as' may be expressed in several ways, e.g. כַּדָּבָר הַזֶּה, 'such a thing as this' (Gn 44:7), גּוֹי אֲשֶׁר־כָּזֶה, 'such a people as this' (Je 5:9), הֲנִמְצָא כָזֶה אִישׁ, 'Shall we find such a man as this?' (Gn 41:38). The preposition may be repeated to express the meaning 'the same as,' e.g. כְּכֹחִי אָז וּכְכֹחִי עַתָּה, 'My strength now is the same as my strength then'

46

(Jo 14:11); cf. Gn 18:25, I Kg 22:4, II Sm 11:25.

257 Approximation, with numerals, e.g. וַיֵּשְׁבוּ שָׁם כְּעֶשֶׂר שָׁנִים, 'They lived there about ten years' (Ru 1:4); cf. Ex 12: 37, I Sm 9:22.

258 Concessive, with an infinitive (cf. §532), e.g. וַיְהִי כְּדַבְּרָהּ אֶל־יוֹסֵף יוֹם יוֹם, 'although she spoke to Joseph every day' (Gn 39:10).

259 Norm, meaning 'in accordance with,' e.g. כַּמִּשְׁפָּט, 'in accordance with the custom' (II Kg 11:14), כְּחַסְדֶּךָ, 'in accordance with your kindness' (Ps 51:3), אִישׁ כִּלְבָבוֹ, 'a man after his own heart' (I Sm 13:14).

260 Causal, before noun clauses introduced by אֲשֶׁר, meaning properly 'in accordance with the fact that . . .' (cf. §534), e.g. כַּאֲשֶׁר לֹא־שָׁמַעְתָּ בְּקוֹל י׳, 'because you have not obeyed the voice of Yahweh' (I Sm 28:18); cf. II Kg 17: 26, Nu 27:14, Ju 6:27.

261 Asseverative, expressing identity, e.g. כִּי־הוּא כְאִישׁ אֱמֶת, for he is a truly honest man' (Ne 7:2), וְשַׂמְתִּיךְ כְּרֹאִי, 'I will make you a veritable gazing-stock' (Na 3:6); cf. II Sm 9:8, I Sm 20:3, Jb 10:9, Nu 11:1.

262 Temporal, expressing exact point of time, to be rendered 'as soon as,' 'at the very time,' e.g. כָּעֵת מָחָר, 'at this very time tomorrow' (I Sm 9:16); cf. Gn 18:10, 14; with an infinitive (cf. §505), e.g. וַיְהִי כְּבוֹא אַבְרָם מִצְרַיְמָה, 'as soon as Abram entered Egypt' (Gn 12:14). If prefixed to a clause introduced by אֲשֶׁר or שֶׁ· the meaning has weakened to a mere 'when' (cf. §500), e.g. כַּאֲשֶׁר אָמְרוּ, 'when they said' (I Sm 8:6), כְּשֶׁתִּפּוֹל עֲלֵיהֶם פִּתְאֹם, 'when it falls upon them suddenly' (Ec 9:12). Exceptionally the form כְּמוֹ may be followed by a clause without an introductory particle, e.g. וּכְמוֹ הַשַּׁחַר עָלָה, 'as soon as dawn came' (Gn 19:15).

263 Pregnant, resulting from an ellipsis of another preposition. e.g. of בְּ in כִּי כְהַר־פְּרָצִים יָקוּם י׳ / כְּעֵמֶק בְּגִבְעוֹן יִרְגָּז, 'for Yahweh will arise as on Mount Perazim, as in

47

the valley at Gibeon he will rage' (Is 28:21), and of לְ

in לַאֲחֵיכֶם כָּכֶם / עַד אֲשֶׁר־יָנִיחַ יי, 'until Yahweh gives rest

to your brothers the same as to you' (Jo 1:15). But con-

trast כְּבָרִאשֹׁנָה, 'as at the beginning' (Ju 20:32).

264 Of degree, with a noun clause introduced by אֲשֶׁר and fol-

lowed by כֵּן, with the meaning 'the more . . . the more,'

e.g. וְכַאֲשֶׁר יְעַנּוּ אֹתוֹ כֵּן יִרְבֶּה, 'They more they oppressed

them, the more they increased' (Ex 1:12).

The Preposition לְ

265 Expresses motion towards a thing or person, or relation

to something.

266 Terminative in space or time, to be rendered 'to,' 'up

to,' e.g. לָעִיר, 'to the city' (I Sm 9:12), לְאֶלֶף דּוֹר, 'up

to a thousand generations' (Dt 7:9), לְעוֹלָם, 'to eter-

nity,' 'for ever' (II Kg 5:27).

267 Directive, meaning 'towards,' e.g. לְאָחוֹר, 'backwards'

(Je 7:24), לְמַעְלָה, 'upwards' (Ezk 8:2), לְעֵבֶר אֶחָד, 'to one

side' (I Sm 14:40).

268 Temporal, meaning 'towards,' 'by,' e.g. וְהָיָה נָכוֹן לַבֹּקֶר

וְעָלִיתָ בַבֹּקֶר אֶל־הַר סִינַי, 'Be ready by morning, and come up

in the morning to Mount Sinai' (Ex 34:2); cf. Ps 90:6,

Ex 19:11, II Kg 4:16, Gn 17:21. In late texts לְ may take

the place of a temporal accusative (cf. §56), expressing

duration of time, e.g. לְשָׁנִים שָׁלוֹשׁ, 'for three years'

(II Ch 11:17); cf. II Ch 29:17.

269 For indirect object, e.g. וַיִּתֶּן־לוֹ צֹאן וּבָקָר, 'He gave him

flocks and herds' (Gn 24:35).

270 Possessive, e.g. וַיִּרְאוּ הַצֹּפִים לְשָׁאוּל, 'The watchmen of

Saul saw' (I Sm 14:16); cf. II Kg 5:9. This is required

when the possessor is definite but the object possessed

indefinite, e.g. הִנֵּה רָאִיתִי בֵּן לְיִשַׁי, 'Look, I have seen

a son of Jesse' (I Sm 16:18); cf. I Kg 18:22, Dt 5:9.

271 Of interest, expressing either advantage, e.g. אָרָה־לִּי

אֶת־הָעָם הַזֶּה, 'Curse this people for me' (Nu 22:6); cf.

48

Nu 23:1; or disadvantage, e.g. מִתְאַנֶּה הוּא לִי, 'He is picking a quarrel with me' (II Kg 5:7); cf. I Sm 9:20 (לָהּ), Ju 12:5.

272 Reflexive, restricted to the same person as the subject of the verb (unlike the לְ of interest), and especially common with verbs of motion, e.g. לֶךְ־לְךָ, 'Go off' (Gn 12:1), שׁוּבוּ לָכֶם, 'Go on back' (Dt 5:30); cf. Nu 22:34, Gn 21:16.

273 Of specification, meaning 'with respect to,' e.g. לָכֵן, 'thus,' and לָרֹעַ . . . לֹא־רָאִיתִי כָהֵנָּה, 'I have not seen their like . . . for ugliness' (Gn 41:19); cf. Dt 5:8, I Sm 9:20. Sometimes this takes the place of the accusative of specification (cf. §57), e.g. וְנִסְלַח לוֹ, 'It shall be forgiven him' (Lv 4:26), leading to the use of לְ with a substantive as a variant of the accusative of the direct object of a verb (as regularly in Aramaic), e.g. לִשְׁחֵת לָעִיר בַּעֲבוּרִי, 'to destroy the city because of me' (I Sm 23:10); cf. Dt 9:27, Am 8:9, Jb 5:2, II Sm 3: 30. So also with the verb קָרָא, e.g. וַיִּקְרָא אֱלֹהִים לָאוֹר יוֹם, 'God called the light day' (Gn 1:5); cf. Gn 1:10. Contrast Gn 26:33, and compare the passive verb in Gn 2:23. It may also appear in place of the normal subject of a passive verb, e.g. פֶּן יְבֻלַּע לַמֶּלֶךְ וּלְכָל־הָעָם, 'lest the king and all the people be engulfed' (II Sm 17:16). Probably here belongs the use of לְ to avoid repetition of a preposition, e.g. בֵּין מַיִם לָמָיִם, 'between waters and waters' (Gn 1:6); cf. Dt 17:8, II Sm 19:36.

274 Norm, expressing mode or manner, and meaning 'according to,' e.g. עֵץ פְּרִי עֹשֶׂה פְּרִי לְמִינוֹ, 'fruit-trees producing fruit according to their types' (Gn 1:11); cf. Gn 13:17. This is equivalent in meaning to an accusative of manner (cf. §60), e.g. לְאַט, 'gently' (Is 8:6), לָבֶטַח, 'securely' (I Kg 5:5), לֶאֱמֶת, 'faithfully' (Is 42:3). With an infinitive לְ expresses the equivalent of a gerund (cf. §195). Sometimes the preposition means 'as compared with,' e.g.

49

עַד אֲשֶׁר־דַּק לְעָפָר, 'until it was as fine as dust' (Dt 9:21).

275 Degree, with a construct infinitive, meaning 'enough to
. . .' (cf. §199), e.g. וַיִּתְאַנַּף יְ׳ בָּכֶם לְהַשְׁמִיד אֶתְכֶם, 'Yahweh was angry enough with you to destroy you' (Dt 9:8);
cf. Dt 9:20, II Sm 13:2.

276 Introducing, in the completion of a construct infinitive
(cf. §§192f.). Here it is pleonastic, e.g. יוֹדֵעַ לַעֲשׂוֹת
בַּזָּהָב, 'knowing how to work in gold' (II Ch 2:13), to be
contrasted with לֹא־יָדְעוּ עֲשׂוֹת־נְכֹחָה, 'They do not know how
to do right' (Am 3:10).

277 Purpose, e.g. וַיַּעַשׂ אֱלֹהִים . . . אֶת־הַמָּאוֹר הַגָּדֹל לְמֶמְשֶׁלֶת הַיּוֹם,
'God made . . . the great(er) light to dominate the day'
(Gn 1:16); cf. Gn 22:7, Ju 20:20. It is especially fre-
quent with the construct infinitive (cf. §197).

278 Product, when an action results in a state or condition,
e.g. וְאֶעֶשְׂךָ לְגוֹי גָּדוֹל, 'that I may make you into a great
nation' (Gn 12:2); cf. Ex 7:15, I Sm 15:1, Ex 21:2. It
is very common with the verb הָיָה in the meaning 'become'
(e.g. Gn 1:14). With a construct infinitive it imparts
a gerundive sense (cf. §196).

279 Result, with a construct infinitive (cf. §198), and occasionally with a substantive, e.g. צֹאן לְטִבְחָה, 'sheep
for slaughter' (Je 12:3).

280 Agent, with passive verbs, e.g. הֲלוֹא נָכְרִיּוֹת נֶחְשַׁבְנוּ לוֹ,
'Are we not considered by him as foreigners?' (Gn 31:15);
cf. Ex 12:16.

281 Distributive (cf. §103), e.g. וַתִּפְקְדֶנּוּ לִבְקָרִים לִרְגָעִים
תִּבְחָנֶנּוּ, 'You inspect him every morning and test him
every moment' (Jb 7:18); cf. I Sm 29:2, I Kg 10:22.

282 Assistance or partisanship, meaning 'for,' 'on the side
of,' e.g. הֲלָנוּ אַתָּה אִם־לְצָרֵינוּ, 'Are you for us or for our
enemies?' (Jo 5:13).

283 Asseverative, as in Ugaritic, with a substantive, e.g.
כִּי לַי׳ מָגִנֵּנוּ וְלִקְדוֹשׁ יִשְׂרָאֵל מַלְכֵּנוּ, 'Truly Yahweh is our
shield; truly the Holy One of Israel is our king' (Ps

89:19); cf. Jb 13:12. This is an archaic use, confined
to poetry.

284 Obligation, a rare use (mostly late) meaning 'encumbent
upon' (so עַל, cf. §294), e.g. הֲלוֹא לָכֶם לָדַעַת אֶת־הַמִּשְׁפָּט,
'Ought you not to be familiar with justice?' (Mi 3:1);
cf. I Sm 23:20, II Ch 13:5.

The Preposition עַל

285 Expresses motion or rest on or above something. It was
originally a substantive (cf. II Sm 23:1, Gn 49:25).

286 Locative, to be rendered 'on,' e.g. עַל הָאֲדָמָה, 'on the
ground' (Ex 20:12); 'over,' 'above,' e.g. עַל־הָאָרֶץ, 'over
the earth' (Gn 1:20; cf. Dt 28:23); 'beside,' e.g. עַל־
קִיר הַבַּיִת, 'beside the wall of the house' (I Kg 6:5).

287 Terminative, meaning 'down to/on,' e.g. וַיֵּרֶד הָעַיִט עַל־
הַפְּגָרִים, 'when birds of prey swooped down on the carcas-
ses' (Gn 15:11); cf. Gn 21:14, Ex 20:26.

288 Adversative, expressing disadvantage, e.g. לְהִלָּחֵם עָלֶיהָ,
'to fight against it' (Dt 20:10), מֵתָה עָלַי רָחֵל, 'Rachel
died to my sorrow' (Gn 48:7); cf. Nu 11:13, I Sm 21:16,
Ps 142:4; sometimes to be rendered 'in spite of,' 'although' (cf. §531), e.g. עַל־דַּעְתְּךָ כִּי־לֹא אֶרְשָׁע, 'although
you know that I am not guilty' (Jb 10:7); cf. Is 53:9.

289 Specification, to be translated 'concerning,' 'with regard to,' e.g. וְעַל הִשָּׁנוֹת הַחֲלוֹם אֶל־פַּרְעֹה, 'and concerning
the doubling of the dream to Pharaoh' (Gn 41:32); cf.
Ex 22:8.

290 Norm, meaning 'in accordance with,' 'on the basis of,'
e.g. עַל כָּל־הַדְּבָרִים הָאֵלֶּה, 'in accordance with all these
words' (Ex 24:8), עַל־צִבְאֹתָם, 'according to their (tribal)
hosts' (Ex 12:51), עַל־יֶתֶר, 'abundantly' (Ps 31:24), עַל
הַמִּשְׁפָּטִים הָאֵלֶּה, 'in accordance with these rules' (Nu 35:24).

291 Causal, e.g. עַל־כֵּן, 'thus,' and הִנְּךָ מֵת עַל־הָאִשָּׁה אֲשֶׁר־לָקַחְתָּ,
'You are about to die because of the woman whom you have
taken' (Gn 20:3); cf. Dt 9:18; with an infinitive (cf.

§535), e.g. וַיִּקְרָא שֵׁם הַמָּקוֹם מַסָּה וּמְרִיבָה עַל־רִיב בְּנֵי יִשְׂרָאֵל
וְעַל נַסֹּתָם אֶת־יְ/, 'He called the place Massah and Meribah
because the Israelites had argued, and because they had
put Yahweh to the test' (Ex 17:7); cf. Je 2:35; or with
a noun clause (cf. §534), e.g. וַיִּגְנֹב יַעֲקֹב אֶת־לֵב לָבָן
הָאֲרַמִּי עַל־בְּלִי הִגִּיד לוֹ כִּי בֹרֵחַ הוּא, 'Jacob outwitted Laban
the Aramaean, because he did not tell him that he was
about to flee' (Gn 31:20).

292 Addition, e.g. כִּי־יָסַפְנוּ עַל־כָּל־חַטֹּאתֵינוּ רָעָה, 'for we have
added a wickedness to all our sins' (I Sm 12:19), וַיִּקַּח
אֶת־מָחֲלַת . . . עַל־נָשָׁיו לוֹ לְאִשָּׁה, 'He took Mahalath . . .
to be his wife in addition to his (other) wives' (Gn
28:9); cf. Nu 31:8, 28:10.

293 Accompaniment, e.g. עַל־מְרֹרִים יֹאכְלֻהוּ, 'It is with bitter
herbs that they shall eat it' (Ex 12:8); cf. Ex 35:22,
I Kg 15:20.

294 Obligation, meaning 'encumbent upon,' e.g. וְעָלַי לָתֶת לְךָ
עֲשָׂרָה כֶּסֶף וַחֲגֹרָה אֶחָת, 'I would have been obligated to give
you ten silver pieces and a girdle' (II Sm 18:11; cf.
II Kg 18:14); cf. Pr 7:14, I Kg 4:7.

295 Advantage, meaning 'on behalf of,' 'for the sake of,'
e.g. אֲשֶׁר־נִלְחַם אָבִי עֲלֵיכֶם, 'because my father fought for
you' (Ju 9:17); cf. II Kg 10:3, Gn 19:17, I Kg 2:18.

296 Indirect object, a late use (so אֶל, cf. §300), e.g. אִם־
עַל־הַמֶּלֶךְ טוֹב, 'If it pleases the king' (Es 1:19); cf. Ez
7:28.

The Preposition אֶל
───────────────────

297 Expresses motion towards a person or thing. It is never
used with an infinitive or a noun clause.

298 Terminative, meaning 'into,' 'unto,' e.g. וְלֹא־תָבִיא תוֹעֵבָה
אֶל־בֵּיתֶךָ, 'You must not introduce an abominable object
into your house' (Dt 7:26); cf. Gn 6:18; equivalent to
לְ (cf. §266).

299 Directive, meaning 'towards,' e.g. וַתִּשָּׂא אֵשֶׁת־אֲדֹנָיו אֶת־

52

עֵינֶיהָ אֶל־יוֹסֵף, 'His master's wife looked up at Joseph' (Gn 39:7); cf. I Kg 8:29f., Gn 32:31; equivalent to לְ (cf. §267).

300 Indirect object, e.g. וַיִּקְרָא אֶל־עֲבָדָיו, 'He called to his servants' (II Kg 6:11); cf. Dt 5:1, Gn 20:17, 16:11; equivalent to לְ (cf. §269).

301 Assistance or partisanship, meaning 'for,' 'on the side of,' e.g. מִי מִשֶּׁלָּנוּ אֶל־מֶלֶךְ יִשְׂרָאֵל, 'Who of our number is for the king of Israel?' (II Kg 6:11); cf. Je 15:1, Ezk 36:9; equivalent to לְ (cf. §282).

302 Advantage, meaning 'for the sake of,' 'on behalf of,' e.g. וַיָּנֻסוּ אֶל־נַפְשָׁם, 'They fled for their lives' (II Kg 7:7); cf. I Kg 19:3; equivalent to עַל (cf. §295) and לְ (cf. §271).

303 Adversative, expressing disadvantage, e.g. וַיָּקָם קַיִן אֶל־ הֶבֶל אָחִיו, 'Cain rose up against his brother Abel' (Gn 4: 8); cf. Nu 32:14, Je 21:13, 33:26; equivalent to עַל (cf. §288); cf. also לְ (§271).

304 Accompaniment, e.g. וְלֹא־תֶחֶטְאוּ לַי' לֶאֱכֹל אֶל־הַדָּם, 'You must not sin against Yahweh by eating (meat) together with the blood' (I Sm 14:34); equivalent to עַל (cf. §293).

305 Addition, e.g. הוֹסַפְתָּ חָכְמָה וָטוֹב אֶל־הַשְּׁמוּעָה אֲשֶׁר שָׁמָעְתִּי, 'You have added wisdom and prosperity to the report which I heard' (I Kg 10:7); equivalent to עַל (cf. §292).

306 Specification, meaning 'concerning,' e.g. כִּי־הִתְאַבֵּל שְׁמוּאֵל אֶל־שָׁאוּל, 'but Samuel mourned for Saul' (I Sm 15:35); cf. II Sm 24:16, I Sm 4:19; equivalent to עַל (cf. §289); cf. also לְ (§273).

307 Norm, meaning 'in accordance with,' 'on the basis of,' e.g. אֶל־פִּי י', 'according to Yahweh's command' (Jo 15: 13), אֶל־נָכוֹן, 'assuredly' (I Sm 23:23); equivalent to עַל (cf. §290); cf. also לְ (§274).

308 Locative, meaning 'at,' 'by,' 'near,' e.g. וַיִּשְׁחָטוּהוּ אֶל־ מַעְבְּרוֹת הַיַּרְדֵּן, 'They slaughtered him at the fords of the Jordan' (Ju 12:6); cf. I Kg 13:20; equivalent to עַל

(cf. §286)

The Preposition עַד

309 Terminative, meaning 'as far as,' e.g. וַיָּבֹאוּ עַד־חָרָן,
'when they had come as far as Haran' (Gn 11:31); cf.
I Sm 9:9.

310 Locative, meaning 'near,' 'at,' 'by,' e.g. וַיֶּאֱהַל עַד־סְדֹם,
'He pitched his tents near Sodom' (Gn 13:12); cf. Ju
4:11, Dt 2:23.

311 Temporal, meaning 'until,' e.g. עַד הַיּוֹם הַזֶּה, 'to this
day' (Gn 26:33); also with a construct infinitive (cf.
§508), e.g. עַד שׁוּבְךָ אֶל־הָאֲדָמָה, 'until you return to the
ground' (Gn 3:19); cf. I Kg 18:29 (with introducing לְ;
cf. §276); or a noun clause introduced by אֲשֶׁר (cf. §502),
e.g. וְלֹא־הֶאֱמַנְתִּי לַדְּבָרִים עַד אֲשֶׁר־בָּאתִי וַתִּרְאֶינָה עֵינַי, 'I did
not believe the reports until I came and saw with my own
eyes' (I Kg 10:7), or כִּי, e.g. עַד . . . וַיִּצְבֹּר יוֹסֵף בָּר
כִּי־חָדַל לִסְפֹּר, 'Joseph stored up grain . . . until he stop-
ped keeping count' (Gn 41:49). With the meaning 'by' it
occurs in יוּמַת עַד־הַבֹּקֶר, 'He shall be put to death by
morning' (Ju 6:31); cf. I Sm 25:22; so also with an infinitive, e.g. עַד־אוֹר הַבֹּקֶר, 'by daybreak' (II Sm 17:22).
Rarely it has the meaning of 'during,' 'while' (cf. Aramaic עַד), e.g. מָה הַשָּׁלוֹם עַד־זְנוּנֵי אִיזֶבֶל, 'What peace is
there during Jezebel's apostasies?' (II Kg 9:22); cf.
Ju 3:26, I Sm 14:19. With a negative עַד־לֹא means 'before,' e.g. עַד־לֹא עָשָׂה אֶרֶץ וְחוּצוֹת, 'before he had made
the earth and its expanses' (Pr 8:26; parallelled by
בְּטֶרֶם in v. 25).

312 Degree, meaning 'up to,' e.g. וְעַד־הַשְּׁלֹשָׁה לֹא־בָא, 'but he
did not come up to the three' (II Sm 23:19); cf. I Sm
11:15, I Ch 4:27; so also with an infinitive, e.g. עַד־
הִשְׁלִכוֹ אֹתָם מֵעַל פָּנָיו, 'to the point that he cast them out
of his sight' (II Kg 24:20).

313 Inclusive, in the construction מִן . . . (וְ)עַד, often to

54

be rendered 'both . . . and' (cf. §327), e.g. ‏מִקָּטֹן וְעַד־‎
‏גָּדוֹל‎, 'both great and small' (I Sm 5:9); cf. Gn 19:4,
Ex 9:25; sometimes without ‏מִן‎, e.g. ‏וַיִּתְּנֵהוּ לְדָוִד וּמַדָּיו‎
‏וְעַד־חַרְבּוֹ וְעַד־קַשְׁתּוֹ וְעַד־חֲגֹרוֹ‎, 'He gave it and his mantle
to David as well as his sword, his bow and his girdle'
(I Sm 18:4); cf. Lv 11:42, Nu 8:4.

314 Emphatic, to be rendered 'even,' e.g. ‏לֹא־נִשְׁאַר בָּהֶם עַד־‎
‏אֶחָד‎, 'Not even one of them survived' (Ex 14:28); cf. II
Sm 17:22, Jb 25:5.

The Preposition ‏מִן‎
‐‐‐‐‐‐‐‐‐‐‐‐‐‐‐‐‐‐‐‐‐‐‐‐‐

315 Separative, e.g. ‏כִּי־יִפֹּל הַנֹּפֵל מִמֶּנּוּ‎, 'if someone should
fall from it' (Dt 22:8); cf. Jo 10:7, Dt 30:3.

316 Temporal, e.g. ‏מִיּוֹם דַּעְתִּי אֶתְכֶם‎, 'from the day that I knew
you' (Dt 9:24); cf. I Sm 18:9; so also in the meaning
'after,' e.g. ‏וַיְהִי כְּמִשְׁלֹשׁ חֳדָשִׁים‎, 'about three months later' (Gn 38:24); cf. Ho 6:2, Ps 73:20.

317 Comparative, with an adjective (cf. §76), e.g. ‏מַה־מָּתוֹק‎
‏מִדְּבַשׁ וּמֶה עַז מֵאֲרִי‎, 'What is sweeter than honey? What is
stronger than a lion?' (Ju 14:18); cf. Ezk 28:3. It is
sometimes followed by an infinitive, e.g. ‏טוֹב תִּתִּי אֹתָהּ לָךְ‎
‏מִתִּתִּי אֹתָהּ לְאִישׁ אַחֵר‎, 'It is better for me to give her to
you than for me to give her to another man' (Gn 29:19).

318 Absolute comparative (elative), expressing a quality of
too high a degree, e.g. ‏הֲיִפָּלֵא מֵי׳ / דָּבָר‎, 'Is anything too
difficult for Yahweh?' (Gn 18:14); cf. Dt 14:24, Nu 11:
14; so also with an infinitive, e.g. ‏כִּי־הָיָה רְכוּשָׁם רָב‎
‏מִשֶּׁבֶת יַחְדָּו‎, 'Their possessions were too many for them to
live together' (Gn 36:7); cf. I Kg 8:64.

319 Causal, e.g. ‏הָרִים רָעֲשׁוּ מִמֶּנּוּ‎, 'The mountains quake because of him' (Na 1:5f.); cf. Ex 2:23; with an infini-
tive (cf. §535), e.g. ‏לֹא מֵרֻבְּכֶם מִכָּל־הָעַמִּים חָשַׁק י׳ / בָּכֶם‎,
'It was not because you were more numerous than all the
peoples that Yahweh was devoted to you' (Dt 7:7); cf.
II Sm 3:11; with a noun clause introduced by ‏אֲשֶׁר‎ (cf.

55

§534), e.g. מֵאֲשֶׁר יָקַרְתָּ בְעֵינַי, 'because you are precious in my sight' (Is 43:4).

320 Means, e.g. וְלֹא־יִכָּרֵת כָּל־בָּשָׂר עוֹד מִמֵּי הַמַּבּוּל, 'All flesh shall not again be cut off by the waters of the flood' (Gn 9:11); cf. Jb 7:14. Used rarely also for an agent, e.g. וְאִשָּׁה גְּרוּשָׁה מֵאִישָׁהּ, 'a woman cast off by her husband' (Lv 21:7).

321 Privative, meaning 'deprived of,' 'without,' e.g. בְּצֵל חֶשְׁבּוֹן עָמְדוּ מִכֹּחַ נָסִים, 'In the shadow of Heshbon the fugitives stand helpless' (Je 48:45); cf. I Sm 15:23; with an infinitive, e.g. וַיִּמְאָסְךָ יי מִהְיוֹת מֶלֶךְ עַל־יִשְׂרָאֵל, 'Yahweh has rejected you from being king over Israel' (I Sm 15:26); cf. Lv 26:13; even with a noun clause, e.g. מִן־יְקוּמוּן, 'without them getting up' (Dt 33:11).

322 Source, e.g. אִבְצָן מִבֵּית לָחֶם, 'Ibzan from Bethlehem' (Ju 12:8); cf. Gn 2:7, I Sm 24:14, I Kg 2:15.

323 Relationship: (1) In space, e.g. מִקֶּדֶם לְבֵית־אֵל, 'on the east of Bethel' (Gn 12:8), מִצְּפוֹן לָעִיר, 'to the north of the city' (Jo 8:13), מֵעֵבֶר לַיַּרְדֵּן, 'across the Jordan' (Nu 32:19); cf. Dt 5:8. (2) In time, e.g. מִמָּחֳרָת, 'on the next day' (Gn 19:34), מֵאָז, 'in the past' (II Sm 15:34). (3) Sometimes it is to be rendered 'before,' 'in the sight of' (i.e. from the standpoint of), e.g. וִהְיִיתֶם נְקִיִּים מֵיי וּמִיִּשְׂרָאֵל, 'You shall be free of obligation before Yahweh and Israel' (Nu 32:22), הַאֱנוֹשׁ מֵאֱלוֹהַּ יִצְדָּק אִם מֵעֹשֵׂהוּ יִטְהַר־גָּבֶר, 'Can a mortal be just before God, or a man be pure before his Maker?' (Jb 4:17), שנואה לאדון ואנשים גאוה ומשניהם מעל עשק, 'Pride is hated by the Lord and man; oppression is a crime before both' (Si 10:7); cf. Je 51:5, Ps 18:22, Si 3:18.

324 Partitive, e.g. יָצְאוּ מִן־הָעָם לִלְקֹט, 'Some of the people went out to gather (it)' (Ex 16:27), וַיָּבֵא קַיִן מִפְּרִי הָאֲדָמָה, 'Cain brought some of the fruit of the soil' (Gn 4:3); cf. I Kg 18:5.

325 Emphatic (similar to עַד, cf. §314), e.g. וְעָשָׂה מֵאַחַת מֵהֵנָּה,

'should he do any one of them' (Lv 4:2), חַי־יֹי / אִם־יִפֹּל
מִשַׂעֲרַת בִּנְךָ אָרְצָה, 'By Yahweh, not even a hair of your son
shall fall to the ground' (II Sm 14:11 = I Sm 14:45).

326 Explicative, meaning 'consisting of,' e.g. וַיִּקְחוּ לָהֶם
נָשִׁים מִכֹּל אֲשֶׁר בָּחָרוּ, 'They took wives for themselves, any
one they chose' (Gn 6:2), דְּבַר־מִי יָקוּם מִמֶּנִּי וּמֵהֶם, 'Whose
word will stand, mine or theirs?' (Je 44:28); cf. Gn 7:
22, 9:10, Lv 11:32, I Ch 5:18, Je 40:7.

327 Inclusive, in the construction מִן . . . (וְ)עַד, often to
be rendered 'both . . . and' (cf. §313), e.g. מִנַּעַר וְעַד־
זָקֵן, 'both young and old' (Gn 19:4); cf. I Sm 5:9, Ex
9:25; occasionally followed by the directive הָ in place
of עַד, e.g. מִכֹּל חֹגֵר חֲגֹרָה וָמָעְלָה, 'everyone who could wear
armour and up' (II Kg 3:21).

The Preposition עם

328 Accompaniment, e.g. הוּא וְהָאֲנָשִׁים אֲשֶׁר־עִמּוֹ, 'he and the men
who were with him' (Gn 24:54); cf. Dt 12:23.

329 Locative, meaning 'near,' 'beside,' e.g. וַיֵּשֶׁב יִצְחָק עִם־
בְּאֵר לַחַי רֹאִי, 'Isaac settled near Beer-lahai-roi' (Gn
25:11); cf. Ju 18:3.

330 Possession, e.g. גַּם־תֶּבֶן גַּם־מִסְפּוֹא רַב עִמָּנוּ, 'We have both
straw and fodder in abundance' (Gn 24:25); cf. Gn 31:32.

331 Advantage, e.g. וְאֵיטִיבָה עִמָּךְ, 'that I may treat you well'
(Gn 32:10); cf. Gn 24:12, 26:29.

332 Adversative or disadvantage, meaning 'against,' e.g. אִם־
תַּעֲשֵׂה עִמָּנוּ רָעָה, 'You must do us no harm' (Gn 26:29); cf.
Ps 94:16; sometimes to be rendered 'in spite of,' e.g.
וְעִם־זֶה לֶחֶם הַפֶּחָה לֹא בִקַּשְׁתִּי, 'In spite of this, I did not
claim the governor's food allowance' (Ne 5:18).

333 Co-ordination, meaning 'and,' 'as well as,' e.g. עָם־
עָרֵיהֶם הֶחֱרִימָם יְהוֹשֻׁעַ, 'as Joshua annihilated them along
with their cities' (Jo 11:21).

334 Comparison, e.g. וְנִמְשַׁלְתִּי עִם־יוֹרְדֵי בוֹר, 'I shall be similar to those who go down to the Pit' (Ps 28:1); cf.

57

Jb 9:26.

335 Reciprocal, e.g. וּפְלִשְׁתִּים נֶאֶסְפוּ לְהִלָּחֵם עִם־יִשְׂרָאֵל, 'Now the Philistines assembled to fight with Israel' (I Sm 13: 5); cf. Gn 30:8, 26:28, Jo 22:8.

336 Assistance, e.g. כִּי־עִם־אֱלֹהִים עָשָׂה הַיּוֹם הַזֶּה, 'for he has achieved by the help of God this day' (I Sm 14:45); cf. Da 11:39.

337 Consciousness, derived from the expression עִם־לֵבָב, e.g. וַיְהִי עִם־לְבַב דָּוִד אָבִי לִבְנוֹת בַּיִת, 'It was in the mind of my father David to build a house' (I Kg 8:17; cf. 10:2), כִּי לֹא־כֵן אָנֹכִי עִמָּדִי, 'for I am not thus in my own mind' (Jb 9:35); cf. Jb 10:13, II Sm 6:22.

The Preposition את
_____

338 Accompaniment, e.g. וְנָשְׂאוּ אִתָּךְ, 'They will share (it) with you' (Ex 18:22).

339 Locative, meaning 'near,' 'beside,' e.g. וְהוּא שָׁב מִן־הַפְּסִילִים אֲשֶׁר אֶת־הַגִּלְגָּל, 'while he turned back from the carved stones which were near Gilgal' (Ju 3:19); cf. I Kg 9:26.

340 Possession, e.g. מָה אִתָּנוּ, 'What do we have?' (I Sm 9:7); cf. Gn 27:15, Ju 17:2.

341 Advantage, e.g. כְּכֹל אֲשֶׁר עָשָׂה אִתְּכֶם בְּמִצְרָיִם, 'just like what he did for you in Egypt' (Dt 1:30); cf. Dt 10:21, I Sm 12:7.

342 Adversative or disadvantage, e.g. וְאַתָּה עֹשֶׂה אִתִּי רָעָה, 'You are doing me wrong' (Ju 11:27).

343 Co-ordination, meaning 'and,' 'as well as,' e.g. וְהִנְנִי מַשְׁחִיתָם אֶת־הָאָרֶץ, 'I am going to destroy them as well as the earth' (Gn 6:13).

344 Reciprocal, e.g. וְאִשָּׁפְטָה אִתְּכֶם לִפְנֵי י׳, 'that I may enter into litigation with you before Yahweh' (I Sm 12:7); cf. Is 53:12.

345 Assistance, meaning 'by the help of' (rarer than עם, cf. §336), e.g. קָנִיתִי אִישׁ אֶת־י׳, 'I have acquired a man with

58

the help of Yahweh' (Gn 4:1); cf. Jb 26:4, Ju 8:7.

346 Partisanship, with the meaning 'for,' 'on the side of,' e.g. וַיֹּאמֶר מִי אִתִּי, 'He said, "Who is on my side?"' (II Kg 9:32).

347 Consciousness (cf. §337), e.g. כִּי־פְשָׁעֵינוּ אִתָּנוּ, 'We are mindful of our transgressions' (Is 59:12, parallel to יְדַעֲנוּם); cf. Jb 12:3, Gn 40:14.

The Preposition תַּחַת

348 Actually the bound form of a substantive, often employed in the accusative of manner (e.g. Gn 49:25) or with the preposition מִן of relationship (cf. §323, e.g. Ex 20:4).

349 Locative, meaning 'under,' e.g. תַּחַת כָּל־הַשָּׁמָיִם, 'beneath the whole sky' (Gn 7:19), or 'at the base of,' e.g. וַיִּבֶן מִזְבֵּחַ תַּחַת הָהָר, 'He constructed an altar at the foot of the mountain' (Ex 24:4).

350 Authority or control, e.g. וַיִּצְבְּרוּ־בָר תַּחַת יַד־פַּרְעֹה, 'Let them store up grain under Pharaoh's authority' (Gn 41:35), וְאִם־לֹא שָׂטִית טֻמְאָה תַּחַת אִישֵׁךְ, 'if you have not strayed into defilement while under your husband's authority' (Nu 5:19); cf. Is 24:5.

351 Identity of situation, to be rendered 'in one's place,' 'on the spot,' e.g. וְעָמַדְנוּ תַחְתֵּינוּ, 'We will stay where we are' (I Sm 14:9); cf. II Sm 2:23.

352 Exchange, to be translated 'in place of,' 'instead of,' e.g. וַיַּעֲלֵהוּ לְעֹלָה תַּחַת בְּנוֹ, 'He offered it up as a burnt offering in place of his son' (Gn 22:13); cf. I Kg 11:43, 21:2, Ex 21:23; with a noun clause introduced by אֲשֶׁר, e.g. וְנִשְׁאַרְתֶּם בִּמְתֵי מְעָט תַּחַת אֲשֶׁר הֱיִיתֶם כְּכוֹכְבֵי הַשָּׁמַיִם לָרֹב 'You will remain but a few persons in place of having been as numerous as the stars in the sky' (Dt 28:62).

353 Causal, with noun clauses introduced by אֲשֶׁר (cf. §534), e.g. תַּחַת אֲשֶׁר קִנֵּא לֵאלֹהָיו, 'because he was zealous for his God' (Nu 25:13); cf. II Kg 22:17; or by כִּי, e.g. וְתַחַת כִּי אָהַב אֶת־אֲבֹתֶיךָ, 'because he loved your (fore)fathers'

(Dt 4:37).

The Preposition בְּעַד

354   The bound form of the substantive בַּעַד (Ca 4:1, 3; 6:7).

355   Locative, meaning 'behind,' e.g. וַיִּסְגְּרוּ בַּעֲדָם, 'They shut (the door) behind them' (Ju 9:51), or even 'through,' e.g. וַתּוֹרִדֵם בַּחֶבֶל בְּעַד הַחַלּוֹן, 'She let them down by a rope through a window' (Jo 2:15); cf. Ju 5:28.

356   Advantage, meaning 'on behalf of,' e.g. וְאֶתְפַּלֵּל בַּעַדְכֶם אֶל־ יְי, 'that I may intercede with Yahweh on your behalf' (I Sm 7:5); cf. I Sm 7:9, Ex 32:30.

The Preposition אַחֲרֵי/אַחַר

357   Probably the bound form of a substantive (II Sm 2:23; meaning 'butt'?); with suffixes the plural form is always employed.

358   Locative, meaning 'behind,' 'after,' e.g. וַיֵּלֶךְ יוֹסֵף אַחַר אֶחָיו, 'Joseph went after his brothers' (Gn 37:17); cf. II Kg 13:2, Dt 11:28, I Sm 14:13. It was an easy transition from the meaning 'after' to 'in the retinue of,' and thence to 'with,' e.g. Ne 3:16-31 (where אַחֲרָיו is parallelled by עַל־יָדוֹ), Dt 23:15, Am 7:15.

359   Direction, with the meaning 'west of,' e.g. וַיִּנְהַג אֶת־ הַצֹּאן אַחַר הַמִּדְבָּר, 'He led his flock to the west of the wilderness' (Ex 3:1), הִנֵּה אַחֲרֵי קִרְיַת יְעָרִים, 'It is west of Kiriath-jearim' (Ju 18:12); cf. Jo 8:2, Ezk 41:15, Dt 11:30.

360   Temporal, meaning 'after,' e.g. אַחַר הַדְּבָרִים הָאֵלֶּה, 'after these things' (Gn 15:1), וְגַם אַחֲרֵי־כֵן, 'and also afterwards' (Gn 6:4); cf. Gn 9:28; with an infinitive (cf. §506), e.g. אַחֲרֵי הִפָּרֶד־לוֹט מֵעִמּוֹ, 'after Lot had parted from him' (Gn 13:14); cf. I Kg 13:23; with a noun clause (cf. §501), e.g. וַיְהִי אַחַר דִּבֶּר יְי / אֶת־הַדְּבָרִים הָאֵלֶּה, 'after Yahweh had spoken these words' (Jb 42:7); cf. I Sm 5:9. This may also be introduced by אֲשֶׁר, e.g. אַחֲרֵי אֲשֶׁר־כָּרְתוּ דזן

לָהֶם בְּרִית, 'after they had made a covenant with them' (Jo 9:16).

361 Adversative, meaning 'against,' e.g. אַחֲרֶיךָ רֹאשׁ הֵנִיעָה בַּת יְרוּשָׁלִַם, 'The daughter Jerusalem has wagged her head at you' (II Kg 19:21); cf. I Kg 14:10, 21:21.

362 Norm, meaning 'in accordance with,' 'after the manner of,' e.g. וַיִּסְפֹּר שְׁלֹמֹה כָּל־הָאֲנָשִׁים הַגֵּרִים . . . אַחֲרֵי הַסְּפָר אֲשֶׁר סְפָרָם דָּוִיד אָבִיו, 'Solomon made a count of all the aliens . . . in accordance with the count which his father David had made' (II Ch 2:16); cf. Is 65:2, Ezk 13:3.

The Preposition יַעַן

363 Also the bound form of an original substantive. Always in a causal sense: rarely with substantives, e.g. יַעַן כָּל־תּוֹעֲבֹתָיִךְ, 'because of all your abominable acts' (Ezk 5:9); with an infinitive (cf. §535), e.g. יַעַן הִתְמַכֶּרְךָ לַעֲשׂוֹת הָרַע, 'because you have prostituted yourself to do evil' (I Kg 21:20); with a noun clause (cf. §534), e.g. יַעַן לֹא־הֶאֱמַנְתֶּם בִּי, 'because you did not believe in me' (Nu 20:12), which may be introduced by אֲשֶׁר (e.g. Gn 22:16) or כִּי (e.g. Nu 11:20).

The Preposition לְמַעַן

364 A compound formed of a preposition and a substantive.

365 Advantage, meaning 'for the sake of,' e.g. וְלֹא־תִשָּׂא לַמָּקוֹם לְמַעַן חֲמִשִּׁים הַצַּדִּיקִם אֲשֶׁר בְּקִרְבָּהּ, 'and would you not forgive the place for the sake of the fifty righteous who are in it?' (Gn 18:24); cf. Dt 30:6.

366 Causal, with the meaning 'on account of,' e.g. וַיִּתְעַבֵּר יְ׳ בִּי לְמַעַנְכֶם, 'Yahweh was angry with me on account of you' (Dt 3:26); cf. I Kg 11:39.

367 Purpose (cf. §197), with an infinitive (cf. §520), e.g. וְיֵהוּא עָשָׂה בְעָקְבָה לְמַעַן הַאֲבִיד אֶת־עֹבְדֵי הַבָּעַל, 'But Jehu acted with cunning in order to destroy the servants of Baal' (II Kg 10:19); cf. Gn 37:22; with a noun clause and the

61

imperfect aspect (cf. §521), e.g. לְמַעַן יִיטַב־לִי בַעֲבוּרֵךְ, 'that it may go well with me because of you' (Gn 12:13), often introduced by אֲשֶׁר, e.g. לְמַעַן אֲשֶׁר אֶרְאֶה, 'that I may watch' (II Sm 13:5); in the negative with לֹא, e.g. לְמַעַן אֲשֶׁר לֹא־יִקְרַב אִישׁ זָר, 'that no stranger may approach' (Nu 17:5).

368 Result, a rare use (cf. §§198, 526), with an infinitive, e.g. וַיְקַטְּרוּ לֵאלֹהִים אֲחֵרִים לְמַעַן הַכְעִיסֵנִי, 'They burned incense to alien gods, thus provoking me to anger' (II Kg 22:17).

The Preposition לִפְנֵי
_____

369 A compound formed of a preposition and a substantive in the bound form.

370 Locative, meaning 'before,' 'in front of,' e.g. וְאַבְרָהָם עוֹדֶנּוּ עֹמֵד לִפְנֵי י׳, 'while Abraham was still standing before Yahweh' (Gn 18:22).

371 Temporal, meaning 'before,' e.g. שְׁנָתַיִם לִפְנֵי הָרַעַשׁ, 'two years before the earthquake' (Am 1:1); with an infinitive (cf. §507), e.g. לִפְנֵי שַׁחֵת י׳ אֶת־סְדֹם וְאֶת־עֲמֹרָה, 'before Yahweh destroyed Sodom and Gomorrah' (Gn 13:10).

372 Mental, meaning 'in the sight of,' e.g. כִּי־אֹתְךָ רָאִיתִי צַדִּיק לְפָנַי, 'for I have seen that you are righteous before me' (Gn 7:1); cf. I Sm 20:1, II Kg 5:1.

373 Comparison, meaning 'like' (a rare use), e.g. אַל־תִּתֵּן אֶת־אֲמָתְךָ לִפְנֵי בַּת־בְּלִיָּעַל, 'Do not treat your servant as a base woman' (I Sm 1:16); cf. Jb 3:24, 4:19.

The Preposition מִפְּנֵי
_____

374 A compound formed of a preposition and the bound form of a substantive.

375 Locative, meaning 'from (before),' e.g. וַיִּסַּע עַמּוּד הֶעָנָן מִפְּנֵיהֶם, 'The pillar of cloud moved away from before them' (Ex 14:19).

376 Causal, e.g. כִּי־מָלְאָה הָאָרֶץ חָמָס מִפְּנֵיהֶם, 'for the earth

is full of violence because of them' (Gn 6:13); cf. Ex
3:7; with a noun clause introduced by אֲשֶׁר (cf. §534),
e.g. וְהַר סִינַי עָשַׁן כֻּלּוֹ מִפְּנֵי אֲשֶׁר יָרַד עָלָיו י' / בָּאֵשׁ, 'Mount
Sinai was completely in smoke because Yahweh had des-
cended upon it in fire' (Ex 19:18).

2 ADVERBS

377 Hebrew possesses very few adverbs. These are normally
replaced by substantives in the accusative of manner
(cf. §60) or with the preposition בְּ of norm (cf. §252),
e.g. טֶרֶם and בְּטֶרֶם, 'not yet,' the similarly employed
prepositions לְ (cf. §274) or עַל (cf. §290), or the first
element in verbal co-ordination (cf. §223). Substantives
with adverbial endings are often used, e.g. אָמְנָם, חִנָּם,
רֵיקָם, יוֹמָם, שִׁלְשׁוֹם, פִּתְאֹם. For negative adverbs see §§394
ff. A few adverbs of manner are here discussed.

The Adverb גַּם

378 Addition, meaning 'also,' either with a following word,
e.g. וַתִּתֵּן גַּם־לְאִישָׁהּ עִמָּהּ, 'She gave some to her husband
with her also' (Gn 3:6); cf. Gn 24:19, 27:34; or with
a clause, e.g. גַּם כִּי־אָמַר אֵלַי, 'He also said to me' (Ru
2:21). Hence (וְ)גַם . . . גַם, 'both . . . and,' e.g. גַם־
אֲנַחְנוּ גַם אֲשֶׁר־נִמְצָא הַגָּבִיעַ בְּיָדוֹ, 'both we and the one in
whose possession the goblet was found' (Gn 44:16); cf.
I Sm 20:27 (negative).

379 Emphatic, meaning 'even,' 'just,' like Greek καί, e.g.
וְהָיָה אִם־לֹא יַאֲמִינוּ גַם לִשְׁנֵי הָאֹתוֹת הָאֵלֶּה, 'if they will not
believe even these two signs' (Ex 4:9), וְאָבִי רְאֵה גַם רְאֵה
אֶת־כְּנַף מְעִילְךָ בְּיָדִי, 'Look, father, just look at the edge
of your robe in my hand' (I Sm 24:12); cf. Nu 22:33,
Gn 20:4, 46:4.

380 Rhetorical, e.g. גַּם־בָּרוּךְ יִהְיֶה, 'Yes, and he shall be
blessed!' (Gn 27:33), מַדּוּעַ רְשָׁעִים יִחְיוּ עָתְקוּ גַּם־גָּבְרוּ חָיִל,
'Why do the wicked live on, grow old, yes, and increase

in wealth?' (Jb 21:7); cf. Is 13:3, Je 6:15.

381 Correlative, meaning 'on one's part,' e.g. גַּם־יְ֒ הֶעֱבִיר חַטָּאתְךָ, 'Yahweh, on his part, has forgiven your sin' (II Sm 12:13); cf. Gn 4:4, I Sm 1:28.

382 Concessive, with the meaning 'although,' 'even though' (cf. §530), e.g. בְּחָנוּנִי גַּם־רָאוּ פָעֳלִי, 'They tested me, although they had seen what I did' (Ps 95:9); so also with כִּי, e.g. גַּם כִּי־תַרְבּוּ תְפִלָּה אֵינֶנִּי שֹׁמֵעַ, 'Even though you offer numerous prayers, I will not listen' (Is 1: 15); cf. §448.

The Adverb אַף

383 Rare in prose, but common in poetry.

384 Addition, meaning 'also,' with a following word, e.g. אַף־אֲנִי בַּחֲלוֹמִי, 'I too had a dream' (Gn 40:16); cf. I Sm 2:7; with a clause, e.g. אַף לֹא אֶל־אֶרֶץ זָבַת חָלָב וּדְבַשׁ הֲבִיאֹתָנוּ, 'Moreover, you have not brought us into a land flowing with milk and honey' (Nu 16:14).

385 Emphatic, e.g. אַף־עַל־זֶה פָּקַחְתָּ עֵינֶךָ, 'Even on such a one you have cast your gaze' (Jb 14:3); cf. Jb 15:4, Gn 18: 13. In a question, this indicates something contrary to expectation, e.g. הַאַף תָּפֵר מִשְׁפָּטִי, 'Will you really impugn my justice?' (Jb 40:8); cf. Jb 34:17.

386 Rhetorical, in poetry, e.g. אַף בַּל־נִטָּעוּ אַף בַּל־זֹרָעוּ אַף בַּל־שֹׁרֵשׁ בָּאָרֶץ גִּזְעָם, 'Scarcely are they planted, scarcely are they sown, scarcely has their stem taken root in the earth' (Is 40:24), יִתְרוֹעֲעוּ אַף־יָשִׁירוּ, 'They shout out, yes, they sing' (Ps 65:14); cf. Is 42:13, Ps 16:6, Pr 23:28.

387 *A fortiori*, with the meaning 'how much more/less,' fol- lowed by כִּי, e.g. הֵן צַדִּיק בָּאָרֶץ יְשֻׁלָּם אַף כִּי־רָשָׁע וְחוֹטֵא, 'If the righteous is recompensed on earth, how much more the wicked and the sinner!' (Pr 11:31); cf. Jb 9:14, 15:16, I Kg 8:27, I Sm 14:30. This כִּי is omitted when a second one follows, e.g. וְאַף כִּי־אָמַר אֵלֶיךָ רְחַץ וּטְהָר, 'How much

64

more, when he says to you, "Wash and be clean!"' (II Kg 5:13); cf. I Sm 23:3, II Sm 4:11.

The Adverb אַךְ

388 Restrictive, meaning 'only,' with a following word, e.g. אַל־נָא יִחַר לַאדֹנָי וַאֲדַבְּרָה אַךְ־הַפַּעַם, 'Let not my lord be angry, that I may speak only this once' (Gn 18:32); cf. I Sm 18:8, Je 16:19; with a clause (cf. §559), meaning 'however,' e.g. אַךְ־בָּשָׂר בְּנַפְשׁוֹ דָמוֹ לֹא תֹאכֵלוּ, 'However, you must not eat meat with its life-blood in it' (Gn 9:4); cf. I Sm 18:17, I Kg 17:13.

389 Asseverative, meaning 'surely (i.e. nothing else than),' e.g. אַךְ טָרֹף טֹרָף, 'Surely he has been torn to pieces' (Gn 44:28); cf. I Sm 16:6.

The Adverb רַק

390 Restrictive, meaning 'only,' with a following word, e.g. רַק הַכִּסֵּא אֶגְדַּל מִמֶּךָּ, 'Only in respect to the throne shall I be greater than you' (Gn 41:40); cf. Ex 10:17; with a clause (cf. §560), meaning 'however,' e.g. רַק בַּבָּמוֹת הוּא מְזַבֵּחַ וּמַקְטִיר, 'However, it was on the high places that he was sacrificing and burning incense' (I Kg 3:3); cf. Gn 24:8. It is used redundantly with אַךְ in הֲרַק אַךְ־בְּמֹשֶׁה דִּבֶּר יְ/, 'Is it only through Moses that Yahweh has spoken?' (Nu 12:2).

391 Asseverative, with the meaning 'nothing but,' 'only,' 'surely,' e.g. וְכָל־יֵצֶר מַחְשְׁבֹת לִבּוֹ רַק רַע כָּל־הַיּוֹם, 'since every scheme devised by his mind was nothing but evil all the time' (Gn 6:5); cf. Gn 26:29; with a clause, e.g. רַק־שְׂנֵאתַנִי וְלֹא אֲהַבְתָּנִי, 'You only hate me; you do not love me' (Ju 14:16).

392 Exceptive or limitative, following a negative, with the meaning 'except,' 'but only,' e.g. אֵין בָּאָרוֹן רַק שְׁנֵי לֻחוֹת הָאֲבָנִים, 'There was nothing in the ark except the two stone tablets' (I Kg 8:9); cf. II Kg 17:18.

393 Emphatic, with conditional אָם, meaning 'if . . . just,'
'if only,' e.g. רַק אִם־שָׁמוֹעַ תִּשְׁמַע בְּקוֹל יי אֱלֹהֶיךָ, 'if only
you will strictly give heed to Yahweh your God' (Dt 15:
5); cf. I Kg 8:25.

3 NEGATIVES

394 Double negatives, when they occur, merely add emphasis,
e.g. הֲמִבְּלִי אֵין־אֱלֹהִים בְּיִשְׂרָאֵל, 'Is it because there is no
God at all in Israel?' (II Kg 1:3, 6, 16); cf. Ex 14:
11, Zp 2:2.

The Negative לֹא
_____

395 Objective denial of a fact (like Greek οὐ). Used with
both perfect and imperfect aspects, e.g. וְאֶל־קַיִן וְאֶל־
מִנְחָתוֹ לֹא שָׁעָה, 'For Cain and his offering he had no regard' (Gn 4:5), לֹא־אֹסִף לְקַלֵּל עוֹד אֶת־הָאֲדָמָה, 'Never again
will I curse the soil' (Gn 8:21).

396 Prohibition, with the imperfect aspect (cf. §173), e.g.
לֹא תֹאכַל מִמֶּנּוּ, 'You must not eat of it' (Gn 2:17).

397 With the gerundive use of the construct infinitive (cf.
§196), e.g. וְלֹא לְהִתְיַחֵשׂ לַבְּכֹרָה, 'He is not to be ranked
as the first-born' (I Ch 5:1); cf. Am 6:10, I Ch 15:2,
Ju 1:19.

398 Elliptic (cf. §594), e.g. וַיֹּאמֶר לֹא, 'when he said, "No"'
(Ju 12:5); cf. Gn 18:15.

399 With nominal or adverbial predicates: (1) adjectives,
e.g. לֹא־טוֹב הֱיוֹת הָאָדָם לְבַדּוֹ, 'It is not good for the man
to be alone' (Gn 2:18); cf. Ex 18:17; (2) passive participles, e.g. אֲשֶׁר לֹא כָתוּב בְּסֵפֶר הַתּוֹרָה הַזֹּאת, 'which is
not written in the scroll of this teaching' (Dt 28:61);
cf. II Sm 3:34; (3) substantives, e.g. הֲלֹא יִרְאָתְךָ כִּסְלָתֶךָ,
'Is your reverence (for God) not your confidence?' (Jb
4:6); cf. Jb 9:32, Ex 4:10, Nu 23:19; (4) prepositional
phrases, e.g. לֹא בָאֵשׁ יי, 'Yahweh was not in the fire'
(I Kg 19:12); cf. I Kg 19:11, Jb 28:14.

400 Privative, e.g. הוּא־בֵן לֹא חָכָם, 'He is an unwise son'
(Ho 13:13); cf. Ps 36:5, Je 2:2, Is 10:15; also with the
preposition בְּ (cf. §252), 'without,' e.g. הוֹי בֹּנֶה בֵיתוֹ
בְּלֹא־צֶדֶק, 'Woe to the one who builds his house by un-
righteousness' (Je 22:13); cf. Jb 8:11, Nu 35:23.

The Negative אַל

401 Subjective denial of a wish (like Greek μή). Used with
the precative (cf. §184), e.g. אַל־אֶרְאֶה בְּמוֹת הַיָּלֶד, 'May
I not witness the lad's death!' (Gn 21:16).
402 Vetitive, with the precative (cf. §186), e.g. אַל־תִּירָא
אַבְרָם, 'Do not be afraid, Abram' (Gn 15:1).
403 Elliptic (cf. §595), e.g. וַיֹּאמֶר לוֹ מֶלֶךְ יִשְׂרָאֵל אַל, 'The
king of Israel said to him, "No"' (II Kg 3:13); cf.
Ru 1:13.
404 In an elliptic statement with the לְ of obligation (cf.
§284) and a modal sense: אַל לַמְלָכִים שְׁתוֹ־יָיִן, 'It is not
for kings to drink wine' (Pr 31:4).
405 As a substantive, occurring in only one poetic passage:
וְיָשֶׂם לְאַל מִלָּתִי, 'and make my word nothing' (Jb 24:25).

The Negative אַיִן

406 Properly a substantive (cf. Is 40:17, 23) like יֵשׁ (cf.
§476).
407 In a bound structure with a following genitive, e.g.
וְהִנֵּה אֵין־יוֹסֵף בַּבּוֹר, 'Joseph was not in the pit' (Gn 37:
29); especially with the subjects of participles, e.g.
אֵינֶנִּי נֹתֵן לָכֶם תֶּבֶן, 'I am not going to give you straw'
(Ex 5:10); cf. Gn 39:23.
408 In apposition to a substantive which usually precedes,
e.g. וְאָדָם אַיִן לַעֲבֹד אֶת־הָאֲדָמָה, 'There was no human to till
the ground' (Gn 2:5); cf. II Kg 19:3.
409 Elliptic (cf. §593), e.g. וַיַּעַבְרוּ בְאֶרֶץ־שָׁעֲלִים וָאָיִן, 'They
traversed the land of Shalisha, but there was nothing'
(I Sm 9:4); cf. Ex 17:7.

410 With the gerundive use of the construct infinitive (cf. §196), with the meaning 'it is not possible to . . .' (mostly late), e.g. וְאֵין עִמְּךָ לְהִתְיַצֵּב, 'It is impossible to withstand you' (II Ch 20:6); cf. Es 4:2, Ez 9:15. This construction may be accompanied by the לְ of obligation (cf. §284), e.g. וְאֵין־לָנוּ אִישׁ לְהָמִית בְּיִשְׂרָאֵל, "It is not for us to put any man to death in Israel' (II Sm 21:4).

411 Privative, with בְּ (cf. §252), meaning 'without,' e.g. הוּא יָמוּת בְּאֵין מוּסָר, 'He will die through lack of discipline' (Pr 5:23), or לְ (cf. §274), e.g. וַעֲצֵי אֲרָזִים לְאֵין מִסְפָּר, 'cedar timbers without number' (I Ch 22:4).

The Negative בַּל

412 This word is confined to poetry.

413 Objective denial (like לֹא; cf. §395), with both perfect and imperfect aspects, e.g. אַף בַּל־נִטָּעוּ אַף בַּל־זֹרָעוּ אַף בַּל־שֹׁרֵשׁ בָּאָרֶץ גִּזְעָם, 'Scarcely are they planted, scarcely are they sown, scarcely has their stem taken root in the earth' (Is 40:24), אָמַר בְּלִבּוֹ בַּל־אֶמּוֹט, 'He has said to himself, "I shall not be shaken"' (Ps 10:6); cf. Ps 147:20.

414 To negate nominal or adverbial predicates (like לֹא; cf. §399), either adjectives, e.g. הַכֵּר־פָּנִים בְּמִשְׁפָּט בַּל־טוֹב, 'To be partial in judgment is not good' (Pr 24:23), or prepositional phrases, e.g. וְלִבּוֹ בַּל־עִמָּךְ, 'but his mind is not with you' (Pr 23:7).

415 Subjective denial (like אַל; cf. §401), with the precative, e.g. וּבַל־אֶלְחַם בְּמַנְעַמֵּיהֶם, 'Let me not eat of their dainties!' (Ps 141:4).

416 With a construct infinitive (like לְבִלְתִּי; cf. §423), only in בַּל קְרֹב אֵלֶיךָ, 'so as not to approach you' (Ps 32:9).

The Negative בְּלִי

417 This form is largely confined to poetry.

68

418 Objective denial (like לֹא; cf. §395), with both perfect and imperfect aspects, e.g. עַל־בְּלִי הִגִּיד לוֹ כִּי בֹרֵחַ הוּא, 'because he did not tell him that he was about to flee' (Gn 31:20), אֹסֶף בְּלִי יָבוֹא, 'The harvest will not come' (Is 32:10); cf. Dt 28:55, Is 14:6.

419 With nominal predicates (like לֹא; cf. §399), either adjectives, e.g. בְּלִי מָשִׁיחַ בַּשָּׁמֶן, 'not anointed with oil' (II Sm 1:21), or participles, e.g. בְּלִי נִשְׁמָע קוֹלָם, 'Their voices are not heard' (Ps 19:4).

420 Privative (like לֹא; cf. §400), e.g. יִשְׂגֶּה־אָחוּ בְלִי־מָיִם, 'Can reeds flourish without water?' (Jb 8:11); so with an infinitive, e.g. מִבְּלִי יְכֹלֶת י׳ / לְהָבִיאָם אֶל־הָאָרֶץ, 'because Yahweh was unable to bring them into the land' (Dt 9:28). Often with the prepositions בְּ (cf. §252) or לְ (cf. §274), e.g. בִּבְלִי־דַעַת, 'unwittingly' (Dt 4:42) or לִבְלִי־חֹק, 'boundless' (Is 5:14).

The Negative בִּלְתִּי
_____

421 Privative (like לֹא; cf. §400), e.g. מַכַּת בִּלְתִּי סָרָה, 'an unerring blow' (Is 14:6), בִּלְתִּי טָהוֹר הוּא, 'He is unclean' (I Sm 20:26).

422 Limitative, usually after a negative, meaning 'except,' e.g. זֹבֵחַ לָאֱלֹהִים יָחֳרָם בִּלְתִּי לַי׳ / לְבַדּוֹ, 'Whoever sacrifices to any god but Yahweh alone shall be exterminated' (Ex 22:19); cf. I Sm 2:2; sometimes also with pleonastic אִם (cf. §457), e.g. אֵין זֹאת בִּלְתִּי אִם־חֶרֶב גִּדְעוֹן, 'This is none other than the sword of Gideon' (Ju 7:14). It may occur with a clause (cf. §557), e.g. לֹא־תִרְאוּ פָנַי בִּלְתִּי אֲחִיכֶם אִתְּכֶם, 'You will not see my face unless your brother is with you' (Gn 43:3), sometimes with pleonastic אִם, e.g. הֲיֵלְכוּ שְׁנַיִם יַחְדָּו בִּלְתִּי אִם־נוֹעָדוּ, 'Do two persons travel together unless they have made an appointment?' (Am 3:3; cf. v. 4).

423 To negate construct infinitives, usually with לְ, e.g. צִוִּיתִיךָ לְבִלְתִּי אֲכָל־מִמֶּנּוּ, 'I commanded you not to eat of

it' (Gn 3:11).

424 With the preposition לְ before a clause to express negative purpose, e.g. לְבִלְתִּי תֶחֱטָאוּ, 'that you may not sin'
(Ex 20:20); cf. II Sm 14:14; cf. §§197, 524.

The Negative אֶפֶס

425 Properly a substantive (cf. Is 34:12, 41:12), employed
commonly as a poetic synonym of אַיִן.

426 Privative, with a substantive, e.g. עַד אֶפֶס מָקוֹם, 'until
there is no room' (Is 5:8); cf. II Sm 9:3 (parallel to
יֵשׁ in v. 1), II Kg 14:26; also with בְּ (cf. §252), meaning 'without,' e.g. וַיִּכְלוּ בְּאֶפֶס תִּקְוָה, 'They have come to
an end without hope' (Jb 7:6); cf. Pr 14:28.

427 Restrictive, meaning 'however,' 'only,' e.g. וְאֶפֶס אֶת־
הַדָּבָר אֲשֶׁר־אֲדַבֵּר אֵלֶיךָ אֹתוֹ תְדַבֵּר, 'You are to say only the
word that I tell you' (Nu 22:35); or 'yet,' 'neverthe-
less,' with a noun clause introduced by כִּי (cf. §558),
e.g. אֶפֶס כִּי לֹא תִהְיֶה תִּפְאַרְתְּךָ עַל־הַדֶּרֶךְ, 'However, you will
have no glory on the enterprise' (Ju 4:9).

The Negative מָה

428 Properly an interrogative, but used occasionally like
Arabic mā (cf. §128), e.g. מַה־תָּעִירוּ וּמַה־תְּעֹרְרוּ אֶת־הָאַהֲבָה,
'You must not arouse nor awaken my love' (Ca 8:4; con-
trast 2:7); cf. Jb 31:1.

4 CONJUNCTIONS

429 There are rather few conjunctions in Hebrew. They are
frequently replaced by prepositions with noun clauses.

The Conjunction וְ

430 Co-ordinative, with the meaning 'and,' e.g. וְלַחֹשֶׁךְ קָרָא
לָיְלָה, 'whereas the darkness he called light' (Gn 1:5);
cf. Gn 10:2.

431 Disjunctive, expressing a contrast, e.g. טוֹב וָרָע, 'good

and evil' (Gn 2:17), יוֹם וָלַיְלָה, 'day and night' (Gn 8:22).

432 Adversative, meaning 'but,' e.g. וְנֹחַ מָצָא חֵן בְּעֵינֵי יי, 'but Noah had found favour in Yahweh's sight' (Gn 6:8); cf. I Kg 2:26.

433 Alternative, meaning 'or,' e.g. אַתָּה וּבִנְךָ־וּבִתֶּךָ עַבְדְּךָ וַאֲמָתְךָ, 'you, your son or your daughter, your male or female slave' (Ex 20:10); cf. Ex 21:16. However, in such expressions as שְׁנַיִם שְׁלֹשָׁה סָרִיסִים, 'two or three eunuchs' (II Kg 9:32), the conjunction is not used.

434 Explicative, to be rendered 'even,' e.g. וְהֶבֶל הֵבִיא גַם־הוּא מִבְּכֹרוֹת צֹאנוֹ וּמֵחֶלְבֵהֶן, 'while Abel on his part brought some of the first-born of his flock, specifically their fat portions' (Gn 4:4); cf. I Sm 17:40 (וּבַיַּלְקוּט).

435 Pleonastic, where it is merely stylistic, as in Ugaritic, Arabic and Ethiopic, e.g. וַתֵּשֶׁב תָּמָר וְשֹׁמֵמָה, 'Tamar sat desolate' (II Sm 13:20), עֶבֶד אָבִיךָ וַאֲנִי מֵאָז וְעַתָּה וַאֲנִי עַבְדֶּךָ, 'I was your father's servant in the past; now I am your servant' (II Sm 15:34); cf. Am 4:10, Jb 4:6.

436 Accompaniment, meaning 'with,' e.g. וַיָּשִׂמוּ אֶת־הָאָרוֹן יי / אֶל־הָעֲגָלָה וְאֵת הָאַרְגַּז וְאֵת עַכְבְּרֵי הַזָּהָב וְאֵת צַלְמֵי טְחֹרֵיהֶם, 'They put the ark of Yahweh in the cart along with the casket, the gold mice and the models of their tumours' (I Sm 6:11); cf. I Sm 25:42, II Sm 12:30; so with circumstantial clauses (cf. §494).

437 Comparative, confined to poetry, e.g. הֲלֹא־אֹזֶן מִלִּין תִּבְחָן וְחֵךְ אֹכֶל יִטְעַם־לוֹ, 'Does not the ear test words as the palate tastes its food?' (Jb 12:11); cf. Jb 5:7, 16:21, Pr 25:25.

438 Emphatic, meaning 'and specially,' e.g. הַרְבָּה אַרְבֶּה עִצְּבוֹנֵךְ וְהֵרֹנֵךְ, 'I will greatly increase your labour pains' (Gn 3:16); cf. I Kg 11:1.

439 Sarcastic, e.g. וְהִנֵּה יי עֹשֶׂה אֲרֻבּוֹת בַּשָּׁמַיִם הֲיִהְיֶה כַּדָּבָר הַזֶּה, 'Were Yahweh even to make windows in the sky, could such a thing as this happen?' (II Kg 7:19), וּמִי אֲבִיהֶם, 'and

71

just who is their father?' (I Sm 10:12); cf. II Sm 18:
11, Ju 14:16.

440 Resumptive, introducing an apodosis, e.g. בְּיוֹם אֲכָלְכֶם
מִמֶּנּוּ וְנִפְקְחוּ עֵינֵיכֶם, 'On the day you eat of it your eyes
will be opened' (Gn 3:5), יַעַן מָאַסְתָּ אֶת־דְּבַר יי׳ / וַיִּמְאָסְךָ מִמֶּלֶךְ,
'Because you have rejected the word of Yahweh, he has
rejected you as king' (I Sm 15:23); cf. Gn 18:26, 32:19.

441 Adjunctive, meaning 'also,' e.g. וְשַׁאֲלִי־לוֹ אֶת־הַמְּלוּכָה,
'Ask for him the kingdom also!' (I Kg 2:22); cf. Nu 34:6.

442 Distributive (cf. §101), e.g. זִקְנֵי עִיר וָעִיר, 'the elders
of each city' (Ez 10:14); cf. Dt 32:7, I Ch 26:13.

The Conjunction אוֹ

443 Alternative, with substantives, e.g. אִם־עֶבֶד יִגַּח הַשּׁוֹר אוֹ
אָמָה, 'if the ox gores a male or female slave' (Ex 21:32),
or clauses, e.g. אוֹ־בֵן יִגָּח אוֹ־בַת יִגָּח, 'or if it gores a
son or if it gores a daughter' (Ex 21:31).

The Conjunction כִּי

444 Causal (cf. §533), e.g. כִּי עָשִׂיתָ זֹּאת אָרוּר אַתָּה, 'because
you have done this, may you be accursed!' (Gn 3:14);
cf. Gn 6:12f.

445 Temporal (cf. §497), in the meaning 'when,' only in verbal clauses, e.g. וַיְהִי כִּי־הֵחֵל הָאָדָם לָרֹב, 'now when mankind began to multiply' (Gn 6:1); cf. Ju 12:5.

446 Conditional, in real conditions (cf. §515), e.g. כִּי־תִמְצָא
אִישׁ לֹא תְבָרְכֶנּוּ, 'If you encounter any one, you must not
greet him' (II Kg 4:29); cf. II Sm 19:8, II Kg 18:22.
There is one unusual example in an unreal condition (cf.
§517): כִּי אָמַרְתִּי יֶשׁ־לִי תִקְוָה, 'if I were to say that I
have hope' (Ru 1:12), but perhaps this is concessive
(cf. §§448, 530).

447 Adversative, after a negative (cf. §555), e.g. לֹא־תִקְרָא
אֶת־שְׁמָהּ שָׂרָי כִּי שָׂרָה שְׁמָהּ, 'You are not to call her name
Sarai, but let her name be Sarah' (Gn 17:15); cf. I Kg

72

21:15; it is more common with pleonastic אִם (cf. §457),
e.g. לֹא יֵאָמֵר עוֹד שִׁמְךָ כִּי אִם־יִשְׂרָאֵל, 'Your name shall
no longer be spoken of as Jacob, but Israel' (Gn 32:29).

448   Concessive, meaning 'though' (cf. §530), e.g. כִּי־תַגְבִּיהַּ
כַּנֶּשֶׁר קִנֶּךָ מִשָּׁם אוֹרִידְךָ, 'Though you set your nest as high
as an eagle's, I will bring you down from there' (Je
49:16); cf. Ps 37:24.

449   Asseverative, a use originating in oaths, e.g. חֵי פַרְעֹה
כִּי מְרַגְּלִים אַתֶּם, 'By Pharaoh, you are indeed spies' (Gn
42:16); cf. I Sm 14:44, sometimes with pleonastic אִם
(cf. §457), e.g. חַי יי כִּי־אִם־רַצְתִּי אַחֲרָיו, 'By Yahweh, I
will run after him' (II Kg 5:20); hence meaning 'truly,'
'indeed,' e.g. לוּלֵא הִתְמַהְמָהְנוּ כִּי־עַתָּה שַׁבְנוּ זֶה פַעֲמָיִם, 'If
we had not delayed, we would certainly have returned
twice already by now' (Gn 43:10); cf. Ps 37:20, Jb 5:
2, 14:7.

450   Resultative (cf. §527), e.g. הֲכַף זֶבַח וְצַלְמֻנָּע עַתָּה בְּיָדֶךָ כִּי־
נִתֵּן לִצְבָאֲךָ לָחֶם, 'Do you have the hands of Zebah and Zal-
munna in your possession already, that we should give
your army food?' (Ju 8:6); cf. Jb 38:20, II Kg 18:34,
Je 2:5.

451   Nominalizing, introducing noun clauses like Greek ὅτι,
e.g. וַיַּרְא אֱלֹהִים כִּי־טוֹב, 'God saw that it was good' (Gn
1:10); cf. Gn 22:12; sometimes after the prepositions
עַד, עַל, עֵקֶב, תַּחַת, יַעַן. Such a clause may occasionally
follow the interrogative particle thus: הֲ(לֹא) כִּי, with
the meaning 'is it (not) a fact that?' (cf. §487), e.g.
הֲכִי יֶשׁ־עוֹד אֲשֶׁר נוֹתַר לְבֵית שָׁאוּל, 'Is there not still someone left of Saul's house?' (II Sm 9:1); cf. Jb 6:22;
הֲלוֹא כִּי אָנֹכִי צִוִּיתִי אֶתְכֶם, 'Is it not a fact that I have
commanded you?' (II Sm 13:28); cf. I Sm 10:1.

452   Recitative, introducing direct speech like Greek ὅτι,
e.g. וַיֹּאמֶר חֲזָהאֵל כִּי מָה עַבְדְּךָ הַכֶּלֶב, 'Hazael said, "What
is your servant? A dog!"' (II Kg 8:13); cf. I Kg 21:6,
Ex 3:12.

73

453 Conditional, in real conditions (cf. §515), e.g. ־אִם
אֶמְצָא בִסְדֹם חֲמִשִּׁים צַדִּיקִם בְּתוֹךְ הָעִיר וְנָשָׂאתִי לְכָל־הַמָּקוֹם בַּעֲבוּרָם,
'If at Sodom I find fifty righteous in the city, I will
forgive the whole place for their sake' (Gn 18:26); cf.
Gn 31:8. Perhaps, as an exception, in two passages to
introduce an unreal condition: אִם־הִכִּיתֶם כָּל־חֵיל כַּשְׂדִּים
יָקוּמוּ . . ., 'If you were to defeat the whole Chaldaean
force . . ., they would rise up' (Je 37:10) and Ps 50:
12; cf. §517, unless this is the concessive use of אִם
(cf. §§454, 529).

454 Concessive (cf. §529), e.g. אִם־יַעֲמֹד מֹשֶׁה וּשְׁמוּאֵל לְפָנַי אֵין
נַפְשִׁי אֶל־הָעָם הַזֶּה, 'Though Moses and Samuel were to stand
before me, I would not favour this people' (Je 15:1);
cf. Am 9:2-4.

455 Alternative, in interrogative clauses (cf. §544), e.g.
הֲלָנוּ אַתָּה אִם־לְצָרֵינוּ, 'Are you for us or for our enemies?'
(Jo 5:13); cf. II Sm 24:13.

456 Privative, expressing a negative after an oath formula
(כֹּה־יַעֲשֶׂה אֱלֹהִים וְכֹה יֹסִף) whether expressed or implied,
e.g. חַיֶּךָ וְחֵי נַפְשְׁךָ אִם־אֶעֱשֶׂה אֶת־הַדָּבָר הַזֶּה, 'By you and your
life, I will not do this thing' (II Sm 11:11); cf. I Sm
17:55, II Kg 3:14. The affirmative is expressed with לֹא,
e.g. אִם־לֹא אֶת־דְּמֵי נָבוֹת וְאֶת־דְּמֵי בָנָיו רָאִיתִי אֶמֶשׁ, 'as surely as I saw the shed blood of Naboth and his sons yes-
terday' (II Kg 9:26); cf. Jb 1:11.

457 Pleonastic, after עַד (introducing an element of doubt)
with a noun clause, e.g. עַד אִם־כִּלּוּ אֵת כָּל־הַקָּצִיר אֲשֶׁר־לִי,
'until they have completed the whole of my harvest' (Ru
2:21); cf. Gn 24:19; sometimes with the particle אֲשֶׁר,
e.g. עַד אֲשֶׁר אִם־הֲבִיאֹנֻם אֶל־מְקוֹמָם, 'until we have brought
them to their place' (Nu 32:17); cf. Gn 28:15; after כִּי
when adversative or asseverative (cf. §§447, 449) and
after בִּלְתִּי (cf. §422).

458 Optative (cf. §550), rarely in place of לוּ, e.g. ־אִם

74

תִּקְטֹל אֱלוֹהַּ רָשָׁע, 'If only you would slay the wicked, O
God!' (Ps 139:19); cf. Pr 24:11.

The Conjunction לוּ

459   Conditional, to introduce unreal conditions (cf. §516),
whether in the past (with the perfect aspect), e.g. לוּ
חָפֵץ ‏יי‏ לַהֲמִיתֵנוּ לֹא־לָקַח מִיָּדֵנוּ עֹלָה וּמִנְחָה, 'If Yahweh had
desired to put us to death, he would not have accepted
a burnt offering and a cereal offering from our hands'
(Ju 13:23); the present (with a participle), e.g. וְלוּ
אָנֹכִי שֹׁקֵל עַל־כַּפַּי אֶלֶף כֶּסֶף לֹא־אֶשְׁלַח יָדִי אֶל־בֶּן־הַמֶּלֶךְ, 'If I
were feeling a thousand silver pieces in my hands, I
would not stretch out my hand against the king's son'
(II Sm 18:12); or the future (with the imperfect as-
pect), e.g. לוּ־חַיָּה רָעָה אַעֲבִיר בָּאָרֶץ וְשִׁכְּלָתָּה, 'if I were to
send wild animals through the land and they to ravage
it' (Ezk 14:15). The negative is expressed by לוּלֵי/לוּלֵא,
e.g. לוּלֵא חֲרַשְׁתֶּם בְּעֶגְלָתִי לֹא מְצָאתֶם חִידָתִי, 'If you had not
ploughed with my heifer, you would not have discovered
my riddle' (Ju 14:18); cf. II Kg 3:14.

460   Optative (cf. §548), either in the past (with the perfect aspect), e.g. לוּ־מַתְנוּ בְּאֶרֶץ מִצְרַיִם, 'If only we had
died in the land of Egypt!' (Nu 14:2); or in the future
(with the imperfect aspect), e.g. לוּ יִשְׁמָעֵאל יִחְיֶה לְפָנֶיךָ,
'If only Ishmael might live before you!' (Gn 17:18);
or even with the precative mood, e.g. לוּ יְהִי כִדְבָרֶךָ, 'If
only it might turn out in accordance with your promise!'
(Gn 30:34).

The Conjunction פֶּן

461   Before a clause this particle expresses fear or precau-
tion, and is to be rendered 'else,' 'lest,' e.g. וְלֹא
תִגְּעוּ בּוֹ פֶּן־תְּמֻתוּן, 'You must not touch it lest you die'
(Gn 3:3); cf. Gn 24:6, 32:12. Often it is used ellip-
tically (cf. §591), when it means 'beware lest,' e.g.

75

פֶּן־יַסִּית אֶתְכֶם חִזְקִיָּהוּ, 'Beware lest Hezekiah mislead you'
(Is 36:18); cf. Dt 29:17.

5   RELATIVE PARTICLES

The Particle אֲשֶׁר

462   By the tenth century B.C., Hebrew and Moabite had abandoned the use of the true relative pronoun (cf. §129),
substituting for it a particle of relationship אֲשֶׁר, derived from an obsolete substantive meaning 'place' (cf.
Akkadian ašru). Such a procedure is semantically akin
to the use of wo in colloquial German or ποú in modern
Greek as the equivalent of a relative pronoun. The particle was then employed as a 'gap-word,' usually to be
resumed by a later element in the clause such as a pronominal suffix or an adverb.

463   Relative, e.g. אֲנִי יוֹסֵף אֲחִיכֶם אֲשֶׁר־מְכַרְתֶּם אֹתִי מִצְרָיְמָה, 'I
am your brother Joseph whom you sold into Egypt' (Gn
45:4); cf. Ex 3:5, Dt 11:10, Nu 10:29. Sometimes it is
used without antecedent, e.g. יָדַעְתִּי אֵת אֲשֶׁר־תְּבָרֵךְ מְבֹרָךְ
וַאֲשֶׁר תָּאֹר יוּאָר, 'I know that he whom you bless is blessed, and he whom you curse will be cursed' (Nu 22:6);
cf. Ju 1:12.

464   Nominalizing, used like כִּי (cf. §451) and Greek ὅτι to
introduce noun clauses, e.g. וַיַּרְא שָׁאוּל אֲשֶׁר־הוּא מַשְׂכִּיל
מְאֹד, 'Saul saw that he was very successful' I Sm 18:
15); cf. Dt 9:7. This is especially frequent after prepositions.

465   Result, very rarely used like כִּי (cf. §527), e.g. אֲשֶׁר
לֹא־יֹאמְרוּ זֹאת אִיזָבֶל, 'so that no one can say, "This is
Jezebel"' (II Kg 9:37); cf. Gn 13:16, I Kg 3:12f.

466   Purpose, a very rare use (cf. §523), e.g. אֲשֶׁר לֹא־תִגָּלֶה
עֶרְוָתְךָ עָלָיו, 'so that your pudenda will not be exposed
on it' (Ex 20:26); cf. Dt 4:40, Jo 3:7.

467   Recitative, employed like כִּי (cf. §452) and Greek ὅτι

to introduce direct speech, e.g. וַיֹּאמֶר שָׁאוּל אֶל־שְׁמוּאֵל אֲשֶׁר שָׁמַעְתִּי בְּקוֹל יְ/, 'Saul said to Samuel, "I did obey Yahweh's voice"' (I Sm 15:20); cf. II Sm 1:4. This is a rare usage.

468 Causal, introducing a noun clause probably equivalent to an accusative of specification, with the meaning 'in that . . .,' and thus employed like כִּי (cf. §533), e.g. וַיָּמָת בֶּן־הָאִשָּׁה הַזֹּאת לָיְלָה אֲשֶׁר שָׁכְבָה עָלָיו, 'This woman's son died during the night because she lay on him' (I Kg 3: 19); cf. I Sm 15:15, Gn 34:13, Jo 4:23.

469 Conditional, very rarely used in real conditions like כִּי (cf. §446), e.g. אֲשֶׁר תִּשְׁמְעוּ אֶל־מִצְוֹת יְ/, 'if you hearken to the commands of Yahweh' (Dt 11:27, parallel to אִם in v. 28), אֲשֶׁר יִשְׁאָלוּן בְּנֵיכֶם מָחָר, 'if your children ask in the future' (Jo 4:21, parallel to כִּי in v. 6). This is to be construed as a noun clause in an accusative function in the light of אֵת אֲשֶׁר יֶחֱטָא אִישׁ לְרֵעֵהוּ, 'if a man sins against his fellow' (I Kg 8:31, parallel to אִם in II Ch 6:22).

The Particle ·שֶׁ/·שַׁ

470 In north Palestinian and late Hebrew the original relative pronoun ·שֶׁ/·שַׁ was in use, but since it no longer exhibited distinctions of gender or number it may be regarded as a particle (cf. §129). Its uses parallel those of אֲשֶׁר (cf. §462).

471 Relative, e.g. כַּחוֹל שֶׁעַל־שְׂפַת הַיָּם, 'like the sand which is on the sea-shore' (Ju 7:12), מַה־שֶּׁהָיָה הוּא שֶׁיִּהְיֶה, 'Whatever has happened is what will happen' (Ec 1:9).

472 Nominalizing, e.g. וְעָשִׂיתָ לִּי אוֹת שָׁאַתָּה מְדַבֵּר עִמִּי, 'Produce a sign for me that it is you who are speaking with me' (Ju 6:17), וְרָאִיתִי אָנִי שֶׁיֵּשׁ יִתְרוֹן לַחָכְמָה מִן־הַסִּכְלוּת, 'Then I perceived that wisdom had an advantage over folly' (Ec 2:13); cf. Ec 2:14; so also after prepositions, e.g. בְּ (Ec 2:16), כְּ (Ec 9:12, 10:3), עַד (Ju 5:7).

473 Result, e.g. מַה־דּוֹדֵךְ מִדּוֹד שֶׁכָּכָה הִשְׁבַּעְתָּנוּ, 'What is your beloved more than another, that you have thus adjured us?' (Ca 5:9), מֶה הָיָה שֶׁהַיָּמִים הָרִאשֹׁנִים הָיוּ טוֹבִים מֵאֵלֶּה, 'How has it come about that the former days were better than these?' (Ec 7:10).

474 Causal, with a noun clause equivalent to an accusative of specification (cf. §468), e.g. שֶׁאַנִּיחֶנּוּ, 'because I must leave it' (Ec 2:18), שֶׁרֹּאשִׁי נִמְלָא־טָל, 'because my head is drenched with dew' (Ca 5:2).

6 THE ACCUSATIVE PARTICLE אֶת

475 The particle אֶת, which is rare in poetry but normal in prose, serves to introduce a determinated substantive, pronoun or clause when in the accusative function, e.g. בְּרֵאשִׁית בָּרָא אֱלֹהִים אֵת הַשָּׁמַיִם וְאֵת הָאָרֶץ, 'when God began to create the sky and the earth' (Gn 1:1), וַיְבָרֶךְ אֹתָם אֱלֹהִים, 'God blessed them' (Gn 1:22); cf. II Kg 8:5. Occasionally it is incorrectly used with an undetermined accusative, e.g. וַיַּעַשׂ אֶת־בֵּית בָּמוֹת, 'He constructed high place shrines' (I Kg 12:31); cf. II Sm 4:11. It is also employed with the accusative of specification (cf. §57), e.g. חָלָה אֶת־רַגְלָיו, 'He suffered in his feet' (I Kg 15:23); cf. I Sm 24:19; with the emphatic accusative of specification (cf. §58), e.g. וַיַּרְא אֱלֹהִים אֶת־הָאוֹר כִּי־טוֹב, 'God saw that the light was good' (Gn 1:4); with the determinative accusative (cf. §59), e.g. וַיֻּגַּד לְרִבְקָה אֶת־דִּבְרֵי עֵשָׂו, 'Esau's words were told to Rebekah' (Gn 27:42); cf. I Kg 18:13; with the temporal accusative (cf. §56), e.g. מַצּוֹת יֵאָכֵל אֵת שִׁבְעַת הַיָּמִים, 'Only unleavened loaves shall be eaten during the seven days' (Ex 13:7); and likewise with the accusative of material (cf. §53), e.g. וַתִּמָּלֵא הָאָרֶץ אֶת־הַמָּיִם, 'The land was filled with the water' (II Kg 3:20). Note that the particle אֶת occurs with מִי, but is never found with מָה, since the latter is indefinite.

476   Occasionally used in its original function of substantive, e.g. לְהַנְחִיל אֹהֲבַי יֵשׁ, 'thus endowing with wealth
those who love me' (Pr 8:21); cf. Si 25:21, 42:3.

477   Expressing existence, e.g. יֵשׁ נָבִיא בְּיִשְׂרָאֵל, 'There is a
prophet in Israel' (II Kg 5:8), אוּלַי יֵשׁ חֲמִשִּׁים צַדִּיקִם בְּתוֹךְ
הָעִיר, 'Perhaps there are fifty righteous within the city'
(Gn 18:24); so with a noun clause, e.g. וְיֵשׁ אֲשֶׁר יִהְיֶה
הֶעָנָן יָמִים מִסְפָּר עַל־הַמִּשְׁכָּן, 'It would happen that the cloud
would be over the tabernacle for a few days' (Nu 9:20);
cf. Nu 9:21.

478   Expressing possession, with the preposition לְ (cf. §270),
e.g. יֶשׁ־לָנוּ אָב זָקֵן, 'We have an aged father' (Gn 44:20),
יֵשׁ אֱלֹהִים לְיִשְׂרָאֵל, 'Israel has a God' (I Sm 17:46); cf.
II Kg 4:2.

479   Occasionally employed to introduce the pronominal subject of a participle, e.g. לָדַעַת הֲיִשְׁכֶם אֹהֲבִים אֶת־יַ/, 'to
find out whether you love Yahweh' (Dt 13:4); especially
after אִם when the construction expresses intention, e.g.
אִם־יֶשְׁךָ־נָּא מַצְלִיחַ דַּרְכִּי, 'if you are really going to make
my journey successful' (Gn 24:42); cf. Gn 43:4.

480   Expressing obligation, with a construct infinitive, e.g.
הֲיֵשׁ לְדַבֶּר־לָךְ אֶל־הַמֶּלֶךְ, 'Ought one to speak on your behalf
to the king?' (II Kg 4:13); cf. II Ch 25:9. This is a
variant of the gerundive use of the construct infinitive
(cf. §196).

481   Elliptic, e.g. וַתֹּאמַרְנָה יֵשׁ, 'They said, "He is"' (I Sm
9:12); cf. II Kg 10:15.

V Syntax of Clauses

482   The Semitic languages, in contrast to the Indo-European
languages, commonly express logical subordination simply
by grammatical co-ordination, i.e. parataxis.

1 NOUN CLAUSES

483   Certain clauses are regarded by native Semitic grammarians as equivalent in function to nouns. Such clauses
may, on rare occasions, be determined by the article
(cf. §91), and when equivalent to an accusative case
may also be marked by the particle אֵת (cf. §475). They
are frequently introduced by אֲשֶׁר (cf. §464) or כִּי (cf.
§451). It should be stressed that the case names merely
express syntactic functions.

Nominative

484   As the subject of a verb, e.g. וּלְשָׁאוּל הֻגַּד כִּי־נִמְלַט דָּוִד
מִקְּעִילָה, 'when it was told Saul that David had escaped
from Keilah' (I Sm 23:13); cf. I Sm 27:4, and often af-
ter וַיְהִי, e.g. וַיְהִי . . . נָתַן יי אֵלַי אֶת־שְׁנֵי לֻחֹת הָאֲבָנִים,
'It happened . . . that Yahweh gave me the two stone
tablets' (Dt 9:11); cf. Is 7:1; more usually introduced
by waw-'consecutive' (e.g. Gn 21:22).

485   In apposition to a nominative substantive, e.g. וְהִנֵּה
אֱמֶת נָכוֹן הַדָּבָר נֶעֶשְׂתָה הַתּוֹעֵבָה הַזֹּאת בְּקִרְבֶּךָ, 'should the report be true and well founded that this abominable act
has been committed among you' (Dt 13:15, 17:4).

486   Equivalent to a predicative nominative, e.g. וְזֶה אֲשֶׁר
תַּעֲשֶׂה אֹתָהּ, 'This is how you are to make it' (Gn 6:15);
cf. Ex 29:38.

487   As subject of an interrogative sentence, e.g. הֲכִי יֶשׁ־
עוֹד אֲשֶׁר נוֹתַר לְבֵית שָׁאוּל, 'Is there not still someone left

of Saul's house?' (II Sm 9:1); cf. Gn 3:1.

488 With an adjectival predicate, e.g. טוֹב אֲשֶׁר לֹא־תִדֹּר מִשֶּׁתִּדֹּור וְלֹא תְשַׁלֵּם, 'That you should not make a vow is better than that you should vow and not make it good' (Ec 5:4); cf. Ec 7:18.

Genitive

489 Clauses in this relationship are always asyndetic. They may occur after a substantive in the bound form, either with introductory אֲשֶׁר, e.g. מְקוֹם אֲשֶׁר־אֲסִירֵי הַמֶּלֶךְ אֲסוּרִים, 'the place where the royal prisoners were confined' (Gn 39:20); cf. Gn 40:3, Lv 13:46, Nu 9:18; or without, e.g. תְּחִלַּת דִּבֶּר־יְ / בְּהוֹשֵׁעַ, 'when Yahweh began to speak through Hosea' (Ho 1:2); cf. Gn 1:1, Lv 7:35, I Sm 25:15, II Kg 8:6; or they may follow a preposition with no introductory particle, e.g. עֵקֶב תִּשְׁמְעוּן אֵת הַמִּשְׁפָּטִים הָאֵלֶּה, 'because you obey these laws' (Dt 7:12); cf. Nu 20:12, Jb 16:17, Am 2:8, Gn 31:20, or introduced by אֲשֶׁר, e.g. אַחֲרֵי אֲשֶׁר הֵנִיחַ יְ / לְיִשְׂרָאֵל, 'after Yahweh had given Israel a respite' (Jo 23:1), or כִּי, e.g. עַל כִּי־עָשׂוּ אֶת־הָרַע בְּעֵינֵי יְ, 'because they had done what was evil in Yahweh's sight' (Ju 3:12).

Accusative

490 As object of a verb, usually with כִּי, e.g. וַיַּרְא יְ / כִּי רַבָּה רָעַת הָאָדָם בָּאָרֶץ, 'Yahweh saw that the wickedness of mankind was great on the earth' (Gn 6:5); cf. Dt 16:12; or אֲשֶׁר (אֵת), e.g. וַיַּרְא שָׁאוּל אֲשֶׁר־הוּא מַשְׂכִּיל מְאֹד, 'Saul saw that he was very successful' (I Sm 18:15); cf. I Sm 24: 11, II Kg 8:5, 12, but occasionally without, e.g. מָה רְאִיתֶם עָשִׂיתִי מַהֲרוּ עֲשׂוּ כָמוֹנִי, 'Whatever you see me do, do the same quickly' (Ju 9:48).

491 In the adverbial accusative of manner (cf. §60), often to be rendered 'by . . .-ing.' Such adverbial clauses are usually asyndetic with a finite verb and inverted word order (cf. §576), e.g. וַיָּבֹא אֲלֵיהֶם יְהוֹשֻׁעַ פִּתְאֹם כָּל־

81

הַלַּיְלָה עָלָה מִן־הַגִּלְגָּל, 'Joshua came upon them suddenly by having marched up all night from Gilgal' (Jo 10:9); cf. Dt 12:22, 7:6, Ex 16:18. In some cases there is no inversion, e.g. וָאֵרֶא וְהִנֵּה חֲטָאתֶם לַי / אֱלֹהֵיכֶם עֲשִׂיתֶם לָכֶם עֵגֶל מַסֵּכָה סַרְתֶּם מַהֵר מִן־הַדֶּרֶךְ אֲשֶׁר־צִוָּה י / אֶתְכֶם, 'I saw that you had sinned against Yahweh your God by making yourselves a molten calf and by quickly turning away from the path that Yahweh commanded you' (Dt 9:16); cf. Dt 7:24. Occasionally the conjunction is used, e.g. וַיַּעֲשׂוּ בְנֵי־יִשְׂרָאֵל אֶת־הָרַע בְּעֵינֵי י / וַיַּעַבְדוּ אֶת־הַבְּעָלִים, 'The Israelites did what was evil in Yahweh's sight by serving the Baals' (Ju 2:11f.); cf. Am 7:12. For such clauses in the negative, either לֹא or אַל may be employed according to the mood desired, e.g. וַיַּעֲשֶׂה הָרַע בְּעֵינֵי י / לֹא סָר מִכָּל־חַטֹּאות יָרָבְעָם, 'He did what was evil in Yahweh's sight by not turning away from all the sins of Jeroboam' (II Kg 13:11), חֲזַק . . . לַעֲשׂוֹת כְּכָל־הַתּוֹרָה . . . אַל־תָּסוּר מִמֶּנּוּ יָמִין וּשְׂמֹאול, 'Be strong . . . to act in accordance with the whole teaching . . ., not deviating from it to right or left' (Jo 1:7).

492 As an accusative of specification (cf. §57), always with אֲשֶׁר (אֵת), e.g. אֲשֶׁר יֵאָמֵר הַיּוֹם, 'as it is said today' (Gn 22:14), אֲשֶׁר בֵּרַכְךָ י / אֱלֹהֶיךָ, 'as Yahweh your God has blessed you' (Dt 12:7), אֲשֶׁר־שָׂם לוֹ בַּדֶּרֶךְ, 'in opposing them in the way' (I Sm 15:2); cf. Lv 26:35. An instructive example is the following: עָשָׂה י / אֲשֶׁר זָמָם בִּצַּע אֶמְרָתוֹ אֲשֶׁר צִוָּה מִימֵי־קֶדֶם הָרַס וְלֹא חָמָל, in which אֲשֶׁר זָמָם is object of the verb, וְלֹא חָמָל is an adverbial accusative, and אֲשֶׁר צִוָּה מִימֵי־קֶדֶם is an accusative of specification, i.e. 'Yahweh has done what he planned, has carried out his promise; as he decreed long ago, he has demolished without pity' (La 2:17).

493 As a determinative accusative (cf. §59), introduced by אֲשֶׁר, e.g. הֲלֹא־הֻגַּד לַאדֹנִי אֵת אֲשֶׁר־עָשִׂיתִי, 'Has my lord not been told what I did?' (I Kg 18:13); cf. II Sm 21:11.

82

2 CIRCUMSTANTIAL CLAUSES

494 Clauses describing concomitant circumstances are introduced by the conjunction וְ of accompaniment (cf. §436), which is occasionally omitted, then the subject followed by the predicate (cf. §582). This may be a participle (cf. §219), e.g. וְהָהָר בֹּעֵר בָּאֵשׁ, 'while the mountain was ablaze with fire' (Dt 5:23); cf. II Kg 8:7, Ex 22:9 (a-syndetic). Other predicates may occur, such as an adjective, e.g. וְהָרָעָב חָזָק בְּשֹׁמְרוֹן, 'while the famine was severe in Samaria (I Kg 18:2), or else a prepositional phrase, e.g. וְהָאִישׁ נֹשֵׂא הַצִּנָּה לְפָנָיו, 'with his shield-bearer before him' (I Sm 17:41), וְרֹאשׁוֹ בַשָּׁמַיִם, 'with its top in the sky' (Gn 11:4), פֶּסַח הוּא לַי /, 'since it is Yahweh's passover' (Ex 12:11, asyndetic and with the copula הוּא).

495 When the circumstances described are past or future, a finite form of a verb is employed. For the past a perfect aspect is used, e.g. וְ/יְ הִצְלִיחַ דַּרְכִּי, 'since Yahweh has made my trip successful' (Gn 24:56), וְהָאָרֶץ הָיְתָה תֹהוּ וָבֹהוּ, 'the earth having been a formless void' (Gn 1:2); cf. Gn 20:4, 26:27, II Kg 3:22. An imperfect aspect expresses a future circumstance, e.g. וְאַבְרָהָם הָיוֹ יִהְיֶה לְגוֹי גָּדוֹל וְעָצוּם, 'since Abraham will certainly become a great and powerful nation' (Gn 18:18).

3 TEMPORAL CLAUSES

496 Simple juxtaposition, meaning 'when,' e.g. וַתְּכַל לְהַשְׁקֹתוֹ וַתֹּאמֶר, 'When she had finished giving him a drink, she said' (Gn 24:19).

497 Introduced by the conjunction כִּי, having the meaning 'when' (cf. §445), e.g. וַיְהִי כִּי אָרְכוּ-לוֹ שָׁם הַיָּמִים, 'when he had been there a long time' (Gn 26:8).

498 Introduced by prepositions followed by noun clauses with or without אֲשֶׁר:

83

499   - בְּ, 'when' (cf. §241), e.g. בְּעוֹדֶנּוּ חַי, 'when he was still alive' (Gn 25:6); cf. Am 4:7. This is never used before a clause introduced by אֲשֶׁר.

500   - כְּ(מוֹ), 'as soon as,' or כַּ(אֲשֶׁר), simply 'when' (cf. §262; with אֲשֶׁר the meaning has weakened since there is no contrast with *בַּאֲשֶׁר), e.g. וּכְמוֹ הַשַּׁחַר עָלָה, 'as soon as dawn came' (Gn 19:15), כַּאֲשֶׁר כִּלּוּ הַגְּמַלִּים לִשְׁתּוֹת, 'when the camels had finished drinking' (Gn 24:22).

501   - אַחֲרֵי, 'after' (cf. §360), e.g. אַחֲרֵי הֵסַבּוּ אֹתוֹ, 'after they had taken it around' (I Sm 5:9); cf. Jo 9:16.

502   - עַד, 'until' (cf. §311), e.g. עַד אֲשֶׁר לֹא־נוֹתְרָה־בּוֹ נְשָׁמָה, 'until there was no breath left in him' (I Kg 17:17).

503   Prepositions governing an infinitive may replace such clauses:

504   - בְּ, 'when' (cf.§241), e.g. בְּעָמְדוֹ לִפְנֵי פַרְעֹה, 'when he entered Pharaoh's service' (Gn 41:46).

505   - כְּ, 'as soon as' (cf. §262), e.g. כְּבוֹא אַבְרָם מִצְרָיְמָה, 'as soon as Abram entered Egypt' (Gn 12:14).

506   - אַחֲרֵי, 'after' (cf. §360), e.g. אַחֲרֵי שׁוּבוֹ מֵהַכּוֹת אֶת־כְּדָר־לָעֹמֶר, 'after he returned from defeating Chedorlaomer' (Gn 14:17).

507   - לִפְנֵי, 'before' (cf. §371), e.g. לִפְנֵי בוֹא־הַשֶּׁמֶשׁ, 'before the sun sets' (II Sm 3:35).

508   - עַד, 'until' (cf. §311), e.g. עַד־שׁוּב אַף־אָחִיךָ מִמְּךָ, 'until your brother's anger withdraws from you' (Gn 27:45).

509   By means of the expression (בְּ)טֶרֶם, 'before,' and a noun clause with the imperfect aspect (cf. §167), either indicating past time, e.g. בְּטֶרֶם תָּבוֹא, 'before you came in' (Gn 27:33); cf. Gn 19:4; or future time, e.g. וְאֶרְאֶנּוּ בְּטֶרֶם אָמוּת, 'that I may see him before I die' (Gn 45:28).

510   By the expression מִדֵּי, 'as often as,' with a noun clause and the imperfect aspect, e.g. כִּי־מִדֵּי אֲדַבֵּר אֶזְעָק, 'as often as I speak, I cry out' (Je 20:8), or simply with an infinitive, e.g. וַיְהִי מִדֵּי־בֹא הַמֶּלֶךְ בֵּית יי, 'as often as the king entered the house of Yahweh' (I Kg 14:28).

84

4 CONDITIONAL CLAUSES

511 The apodosis is usually introduced by the resumptive וְ (cf. §440); note, however, II Kg 4:29, Gn 18:3, etc. Occasionally אָז is used in real or unreal conditions (e.g. Pr 2:5, II Sm 19:7).

Real Conditions

512 By simple juxtaposition (virtual conditional), e.g. וְעָזַב אֶת־אָבִיו וָמֵת, 'Should he leave his father, he will die' (Gn 44:22); cf. I Sm 19:3.

513 By means of a circumstantial clause (cf. §494), e.g. הִנֵּה יי עֹשֶׂה / אֲרֻבּוֹת בַּשָּׁמַיִם הֲיִהְיֶה הַדָּבָר הַזֶּה, 'Were Yahweh to make windows in the sky, could such a thing as this happen?' (II Kg 7:2); cf. Ex 3:13.

514 With the particle הֵן (cf. Aramaic and הִנֵּה in §513), e.g. הֵן צַדִּיק בָּאָרֶץ יְשֻׁלָּם, 'if the righteous is recompensed on earth' (Pr 11:31).

515 With the particles אִם (cf. §453) or כִּי (cf. §446), expressing past time (with the perfect aspect), e.g. אִם־נָא מָצָאתִי חֵן בְּעֵינֶיךָ, 'if I have just found favour in your sight' (Gn 18:3), כִּי שָׂטִית תַּחַת אִישֵׁךְ וְכִי נִטְמֵאת, 'if you have gone astray while under your husband's authority, and if you have become defiled' (Nu 5:20); past frequentative time (with the imperfect aspect), e.g. וְאִם־לֹא יֵעָלֶה הֶעָנָן, 'if the cloud does not lift itself up' (Ex 40:37); future time (with the imperfect aspect), e.g. אִם־יִהְיֶה אֱלֹהִים עִמָּדִי, 'if God will be with me' (Gn 28:20); imminent future or present time (with the participle), e.g. אִם־לֹקֵחַ יַעֲקֹב אִשָּׁה, 'if Jacob is going to marry a woman' (Gn 27:46), כִּי־אֵינְךָ יוֹצֵא, 'if you are not about to go forth' (II Sm 19:8); present frequentative time (with the imperfect aspect), e.g. וְאִם לֹא תֵיטִיב, 'if you do not do well' (Gn 4:7). Very rarely the particle אֲשֶׁר is used (cf. §469), e.g. אֲשֶׁר תִּשְׁמְעוּ אֶל־מִצְוֹת יי, 'if you listen to the commands of Yahweh' (Dt 11:27); cf. Jo 4:21.

85

Unreal Conditions

516   With the particle לוּ(cf. §459), usually in past time (with the perfect aspect), e.g. לוּ הַחֲיִתֶם אוֹתָם, 'if you had let them live' (Ju 8:19); cf. Ju 13:23; the negative is expressed by לוּלֵא/לוּלֵי, e.g. לוּלֵא הִתְמַהְמָהְנוּ, 'if we had not delayed' (Gn 43:10). Rarely in present or future time (with a participle), e.g. וְלֹא אָנֹכִי שֹׁקֵל עַל־כַּפַּי אֶלֶף כֶּסֶף, 'if I were feeling a thousand silver pieces in my hands' (II Sm 18:12); cf. II Sm 19:7; in the negative, לוּלֵי פְּנֵי יְהוֹשָׁפָט . . . אֲנִי נֹשֵׂא, 'if I did not respect Jehoshaphat' (II Kg 3:14). In late times אִלּוּ is used, e.g. וְאִלּוּ חָיָה אֶלֶף שָׁנִים פַּעֲמַיִם, 'if he were to live a thousand years twice over' (Ec 6:6); cf. Es 7:4.

517   Exceptionally with the particles כִּי (e.g. Ru 1:12) or אִם (e.g. Ps 50:12); cf. §§446, 453.

5 TELIC (FINAL OR PURPOSE) CLAUSES

518   By means of 'simple' waw and the precative mood (cf. §187), e.g. וְהָבִיאָה לִּי וְאֹכֵלָה, 'Bring it to me that I may eat' (Gn 27:4); cf. Lv 9:6.

519   By means of waw and the imperative mood (cf. §189), e.g. מָה אֶעֱשֶׂה לָכֶם . . . וּבָרְכוּ אֶת־נַחֲלַת יְ/, 'What may I do for you . . . that you may bless Yahweh's heritage?' (II Sm 21:3); cf. Is 45:22.

520   The preposition לְ and a construct infinitive may take the place of a clause (cf. §197), e.g. וַיַּעֲלֶה אַחְאָב לֶאֱכֹל וְלִשְׁתּוֹת, 'Ahab climbed up to eat and drink' (I Kg 18:42), or לְמַעַן with an infinitive (cf. §367), e.g. לְמַעַן הַצִּיל אֹתוֹ מִיָּדָם, 'that he might rescue him from their clutches' (Gn 37:22).

521   By לְמַעַן with a noun clause (with or without אֲשֶׁר) and the imperfect aspect (cf. §§175, 367), e.g. בְּקוֹל יְ/ . . . נִשְׁמָע לְמַעַן אֲשֶׁר יִיטַב־לָנוּ, 'We shall obey the voice of Yahweh . . ., in order that it may go well with us' (Je 42:6); cf. Gn 12:13.

522 By בַּעֲבוּר with a noun clause (with or without אֲשֶׁר), e.g.
וְהָבִיאָה לִּי וְאֹכֵלָה בַּעֲבוּר תְּבָרֶכְךָ נַפְשִׁי בְּטֶרֶם אָמוּת, 'Bring it
in to me that I may eat it, in order that I may person-
ally bless you before I die' (Gn 27:4); cf. Gn 27:10,
21:30. An infinitive may take the place of such a clause,
e.g. בַּעֲבוּר זֹאת הֶעֱמַדְתִּיךָ בַּעֲבוּר הַרְאֹתְךָ אֶת־כֹּחִי, 'Because of
this I let you remain in order to show you my power' (Ex
9:16); cf. II Sm 10:3 (also pleonastically לְבַעֲבוּר, e.g.
II Sm 14:20, Ex 20:20).

523 Very rarely by means of the particle אֲשֶׁר with a noun
clause (cf. §466), e.g. וְשָׁמַרְתָּ אֶת־חֻקָּיו . . . אֲשֶׁר יִיטַב לְךָ
וּלְבָנֶיךָ אַחֲרֶיךָ, 'You must keep his statutes . . ., that
it may be well with you and your children after you'
(Dt 4:40); cf. Jo 3:7.

524 Negative purpose is expressed by לְבִלְתִּי introducing a
noun clause with an imperfect aspect (cf. §424), e.g.
כִּי לְבַעֲבוּר נַסּוֹת אֶתְכֶם בָּא הָאֱלֹהִים . . . לְבִלְתִּי תֶחֱטָאוּ, 'for
it was to test you that God came . . ., that you might
not sin' (Ex 20:20); cf. II Sm 14:14; or with a construct infinitive in place of a clause (cf. §423), e.g.
וַיָּשֶׂם יְ / לְקַיִן אוֹת לְבִלְתִּי הַכּוֹת־אֹתוֹ כָּל־מֹצְאוֹ, 'Yahweh put a
mark on Cain that any one encountering him might not
strike him down' (Gn 4:15); cf. II Kg 23:10. Rarely,
לְמַעַן (אֲשֶׁר) לֹא with a noun clause (cf. §367) is used,
e.g. לְמַעַן אֲשֶׁר לֹא־יִקְרַב אִישׁ זָר, 'that no stranger may approach' (Nu 17:5); cf. Ezk 14:11.

6   RESULT CLAUSES

525 By means of a simple consecutive sequence (cf. §§178f.),
e.g. וַיִּסְקְלֻהוּ בָאֲבָנִים וַיָּמֹת, 'They pelted him with stones
so that he died' (I Kg 21:13).

526 In place of a clause a construct infinitive may be sub-
stituted, either with לְ (cf. §279), e.g. וּלְחַלֵּל אֶת־שֵׁם
קָדְשִׁי, 'thus profaning my holy name' (Lv 20:3), or rarely לְמַעַן (cf. §368).

527 With a noun clause introduced by כִּי (cf. §450), e.g.
וְאַהֲרֹן מַה־הוּא כִּי תַלּוֹנוּ עָלָיו, 'As for Aaron, what is he
that you grumble at him?' (Nu 16:11); cf. Gn 20:10, or
rarely by אֲשֶׁר (cf. §465), e.g. אֲשֶׁר כָּמוֹךָ לֹא־הָיָה לְפָנֶיךָ,
'so that no one like you has existed before you' (I Kg
3:12).

7 CONCESSIVE CLAUSES

528 By means of a circumstantial clause (cf. §494), e.g.
הִנֵּה־נָא הוֹאַלְתִּי לְדַבֵּר אֶל־אֲדֹנָי וְאָנֹכִי עָפָר וָאֵפֶר, 'Here I have
undertaken to speak to the Lord, though I am but dust
and ashes' (Gn 18:27); cf. Ju 16:15.

529 By means of the conjunction אִם (cf. §454), e.g. אִם־צָדַקְתִּי
לֹא אֶעֱנֶה, 'Though I am innocent, I cannot reply' (Jb 9:
15); cf. Am 9:2-4.

530 By means of גַם כִּי, e.g. גַם כִּי־תַרְבּוּ תְפִלָּה אֵינֶנִּי שֹׁמֵעַ, 'Even
though you offer numerous prayers, I will not listen'
(Is 1:15), or simply כִּי (cf. §448), e.g. כִּי־תַעֲלֶה בָבֶל
הַשָּׁמַיִם וְכִי תְבַצֵּר מְרוֹם עֻזָּהּ, 'though Babylon should climb
to the sky, and though she should fortify her strong
aerie' (Je 51:53), or גַם (cf. §382), e.g. רַבַּת צְרָרוּנִי
מִנְּעוּרַי גַּם לֹא־יָכְלוּ לִי, 'Greatly have they harassed me
since my youth, though they have not overcome me' (Ps
129:2).

531 By means of the preposition עַל with a noun clause (cf.
§288), e.g. עַל לֹא־חָמָס עָשָׂה, 'although he had perpetrated
no violence' (Is 53:9); cf. Jb 16:17, or with an infinitive instead of a clause, e.g. עַל־דַּעְתְּךָ כִּי־לֹא אֶרְשָׁע, 'although you know that I am not guilty' (Jb 10:7).

532 The preposition בְּ (cf. §258) with an infinitive may replace a concessive clause, e.g. וַיְהִי כְּדַבְּרָהּ אֶל־יוֹסֵף יוֹם
יוֹם, 'now although she spoke to Joseph every day' (Gn
39:10).

8 CAUSAL CLAUSES

533 By means of the conjunction כִּי (cf. §444), e.g. ‏קֵץ כָּל־‏ בָּשָׂר בָּא לְפָנַי כִּי־מָלְאָה הָאָרֶץ חָמָס מִפְּנֵיהֶם, 'I have decided on an end to all flesh, for the earth is full of violence because of them' (Gn 6:13), or the particle אֲשֶׁר (cf. §468), e.g. מֵעֲמָלֵקִי הֱבִיאוּם אֲשֶׁר חָמַל הָעָם עַל־מֵיטַב הַצֹּאן וְהַבָּקָר, 'It was from the Amalekites that they brought them, because the people spared the best of the flocks and herds' (I Sm 15:15); cf. II Sm 2:5.

534 By use of a preposition followed by a noun clause, viz. יַעַן (אֲשֶׁר/כִּי) (cf. §363), e.g. יַעַן כִּי גָבְהוּ בְּנוֹת צִיּוֹן, 'because the women of Zion are haughty' (Is 3:16); cf. Nu 20:12, Gn 22:16; עַל (אֲשֶׁר/כִּי) (cf. §291), e.g. ‏עַל לֹא־‏ שָׁמְרוּ תוֹרָתֶךָ, 'because they have not observed your teaching' (Ps 119:136); cf. II Sm 3:30, Ju 3:12; בַּ(אֲשֶׁר) (cf. §247), e.g. בַּאֲשֶׁר י/ אִתּוֹ, 'because Yahweh was with him' (Gn 39:23); cf. Gn 39:9; כַּ(אֲשֶׁר) (cf. §260), e.g. וְהִנָּם מְמִיתִים אוֹתָם כַּאֲשֶׁר אֵינָם יֹדְעִים אֶת־מִשְׁפַּט אֱלֹהֵי הָאָרֶץ, 'Here they are killing them, because they do not know the usage of the god of the land' (II Kg 17:26); cf. I Sm 28:18, Nu 27:14; מֵ(אֲשֶׁר) (cf. §319), e.g. מֵאֲשֶׁר יָקַרְתָּ בְעֵינַי, 'because you are precious in my sight' (Is 43:4); עֵקֶב (אֲשֶׁר/כִּי), e.g. עֵקֶב הָיְתָה רוּחַ אַחֶרֶת עִמּוֹ, 'because he had a different spirit' (Nu 14:24); cf. Gn 22:18, II Sm 12:10; תַּחַת (אֲשֶׁר/כִּי) (cf. §353), e.g. תַּחַת כִּי־שָׂנְאוּ דָעַת, 'because they hated knowledge' (Pr 1:29); cf. Nu 25:13, II Kg 22:17; מִפְּנֵי (אֲשֶׁר) (cf. §376), e.g. מִפְּנֵי אֲשֶׁר קִטַּרְתֶּם, 'in view of the fact that you burned sacrifices' (Je 44:23); cf. Ex 19:18.

535 The equivalent of a causal clause may be expressed by means of a preposition with a construct infinitive, viz. יַעַן (cf. §363), e.g. יַעַן הִתְרַגֶּזְךָ אֵלַי, 'because of your frenzied raging against me' (II Kg 19:28 = Is 37:29); cf. I Kg 21:20; עַל (cf. §291), e.g. ‏עַל־מִכְרָם בַּכֶּסֶף צַדִּיק‏,

'because they sold the righteous for silver' (Am 2:6); cf. Am 1:9; בְּ (cf. §247), e.g. הֲלוֹא בְּלֶכְתְּךָ עִמָּנוּ, 'Is it not because of your accompanying us?' (Ex 33:16); cf. I Kg 18:18; מִן (cf. §319), e.g. מִיִּרְאָתוֹ אֹתוֹ, 'because he was afraid of him' (II Sm 3:11); cf. Dt 7:7.

9 RELATIVE CLAUSES

536 Occasionally in poetry introduced by the obsolescent relative pronouns זוּ, זוֹ, זֶה (cf. §129), e.g. בְּרֶשֶׁת־זוּ טָמָנוּ, 'in the net which they concealed' (Ps 9:16); cf. Jb 19:19.

537 In north Palestinian and late Hebrew introduced by the dialectal relative pronoun ־שֶׁ (cf. §§129, 470f.), e.g. מִי מִשֶּׁלָּנוּ, 'Who that is of our number?' (II Kg 6:11); cf. Ju 7:12, Ec 1:9.

538 Usually (although rarely in poetry) by means of the relative particle אֲשֶׁר (cf. §§462f.), e.g. הַמָּקוֹם אֲשֶׁר אַתָּה עוֹמֵד עָלָיו, 'the place upon which you are standing' (Ex 3:5).

539 By means of the article before a participle (cf. §90), e.g. וְאֶל־מֶלֶךְ יְהוּדָה הַשֹּׁלֵחַ אֶתְכֶם לִדְרֹשׁ אֶת־יְ׳, 'to the king of Judah who is sending you to consult Yahweh' (II Kg 22:18); cf. Is 8:6; or a clause with a finite verb (cf. §91), e.g. הַנִּרְאָה אֵלָיו פַּעֲמָיִם, 'who had appeared to him twice' (I Kg 11:9); cf. Ez 10:17.

540 By means of parataxis or simple juxtaposition of clauses (i.e. virtual relative), a construction common in poetry and originally employed when the antecedent was indefinite (as in Arabic). An example is יֹאבַד יוֹם אִוָּלֶד בּוֹ, וְהַלַּיְלָה אָמַר הֹרָה גָבֶר, 'Perish the day in which I was born, and the night which said, "A man has been conceived"!' (Jb 3:3); cf. Dt 32:17, Is 40:20, Je 13:20, Ps 18:44. This is occasionally found also in prose, e.g. אֶת־הַדֶּרֶךְ יֵלְכוּ בָהּ, 'the path on which they are to proceed' (Ex 18:20); cf. Gn 15:13.

90

541 Direct questions are introduced by the particle הֲ, e.g.
הֲתֵלְכִי עִם־הָאִישׁ הַזֶּה, 'Will you go with this man?' (Gn 24:
58); cf. Gn 50:19.

542 Sometimes they are expressed merely by intonation, e.g.
וַיֹּאמֶר שָׁלֹם בּוֹאֶךָ, 'They (Heb. he) said, "Is your coming
peaceable?"' (I Sm 16:4); cf. I Sm 11:12, II Sm 11:11.

543 Indirect questions are indicated by הֲ, e.g. לָדַעַת הֲיִשְׁכֶם
אֹהֲבִים אֶת־יְ/ אֱלֹהֵיכֶם, 'to find out whether you love Yahweh your God' (Dt 13:4), or אִם, e.g. אִם־ . . . לְכוּ דִרְשׁוּ
אֶחְיֶה מֵחֳלִי זֶה, 'Go, inquire . . . whether I shall recover
from this illness <of mine>'(II Kg 1:2).

544 Disjunctive questions are expressed by (וְ)אִם . . . הֲ,
e.g. הַכֶּר־נָא הַכְּתֹנֶת בִּנְךָ הִוא אִם־לֹא, 'Just ascertain whether
it is your son's tunic or not' (Gn 37:32); cf. Jb 22:3;
less frequently by הֲ . . . הֲ, e.g. הֶחָזָק הוּא הֲרָפֶה, 'whether it is strong or weak' (Nu 13:18); or still more
rarely by אוֹ . . . הֲ, e.g. וּמִי יוֹדֵעַ הֶחָכָם יִהְיֶה אוֹ סָכָל,
'Who knows whether he will be a wise man or a fool?'
(Ec 2:19); cf. Ju 18:19.

545 Interrogative pronouns or adverbs may be employed, such
as מִי, 'who?' מָה, 'what?' אָן, 'where?' אֵיךְ, 'how?'

11 DESIDERATIVE (OPTATIVE) CLAUSES

546 Expressed by the precative mood (cf. §184), e.g. אָשִׂימָה
עָלַי מֶלֶךְ כְּכָל־הַגּוֹיִם, 'Let me set a king over me as all
the nations do!' (Dt 17:14); cf. I Sm 1:23.

547 By means of מִי־יִתֵּן with a perfect aspect, e.g. מִי־יִתֵּן
יָדַעְתִּי וְאֶמְצָאֵהוּ, 'If only I knew how to find him!' (Jb
23:3); an imperfect aspect, e.g. מִי יִתֵּן בִּשְׁאוֹל תַּצְפִּנֵנִי,
'If only you would hide me in Sheol!' (Jb 14:13); cf.
Jb 6:8; in this case the main verb may be introduced by
waw-'consecutive,' e.g. . . . וּמִי־יִתֵּן וְהָיָה לְבָבָם זֶה לָהֶם
כָּל־הַיָּמִים, 'If only they would have this mind of theirs

always!' (Dt 5:29). Occasionally מִי־יִתֵּן may occur in a
non-verbal clause, e.g. וּמִי יִתֵּן כָּל־עַם יְ / נְבִיאִים, 'If
only all Yahweh's people were prophets!' (Nu 11:29);
cf. Dt 28:67. So with a construct infinitive, e.g. מִי־
יִתֵּן מוּתִי אֲנִי תַחְתֶּיךָ, 'If only I myself had died instead
of you!' (II Sm 19:1); cf. Ex 16:3. Sometimes מִי alone
is used (cf. §122), e.g. מִי יַשְׁקֵנִי מַיִם, 'If only someone
would give me a drink of water!' (II Sm 23:15); cf. II
Sm 15:4.

548   By means of לוּ (cf. §460) with the imperfect aspect,
e.g. לוּ שָׁקוֹל יִשָּׁקֵל כַּעְשִׂי, 'If only my vexation might be
weighed out!' (Jb 6:2); cf. Gn 17:18; with the perfect
aspect, e.g. וְלוּ הוֹאַלְנוּ וַנֵּשֶׁב בְּעֵבֶר הַיַּרְדֵּן, 'If only we
had been content to settle on the other side of the Jor-
dan!' (Jo 7:7); cf. Nu 14:2; with the precative mood,
e.g. לוּ יְהִי כִדְבָרֶךָ, 'If only it might turn out according
to your promise!' (Gn 30:34); also in an existential
sentence, e.g. לוּ יֶשׁ־חֶרֶב בְּיָדִי, 'If only there were a
sword in my hand!' (Nu 22:29).

549   By means of אַחֲלֵי/אַחֲלַי/אַחֲלֵי, e.g. אַחֲלֵי אֲדֹנִי לִפְנֵי הַנָּבִיא אֲשֶׁר
בְּשֹׁמְרוֹן, 'If only my master were in the presence of the
prophet who is in Samaria!' (II Kg 5:3); cf. Ps 119:5.

550   Rarely by means of אִם (cf. §458), e.g. אִם־תִּקְטֹל אֱלוֹהַּ רָשָׁע,
'If only you would slay the wicked, O God!' (Ps 139:19).

551   A wish may also be expressed by means of a non-verbal
clause. The predicate may be a noun, e.g. עֵד הַגַּל הַזֶּה,
'Let this cairn be a witness!' (Gn 31:52), a participle,
e.g. בָּרוּךְ בְּנִי לַי /, 'May my son be blessed by Yahweh!'
(Ju 17:2), or a prepositional phrase, e.g. חַג לַי / מָחָר,
'Let there be a festival for Yahweh tomorrow!' (Ex 32:
5). For the word order see §580.

12   ADVERSATIVE CLAUSES

552   Introduced by the conjunction וְ (cf. §432), e.g. וְלֹא־
יִקָּרֵא עוֹד אֶת־שִׁמְךָ אַבְרָם וְהָיָה שִׁמְךָ אַבְרָהָם, 'Your name shall

92

no longer be called Abram, but your name shall be Abraham' (Gn 17:5); cf. I Kg 3:11.

553 By means of the adverb אוּלָם(וְ), e.g. וְאוּלָם אָחִיו הַקָּטֹן
יִגְדַּל מִמֶּנּוּ?, 'But his younger brother shall be greater
than he' (Gn 48:19); cf. Ex 9:16, Jb 1:11, 2:5.

554 The particle אֲבָל (only asseverative in classical Hebrew)
is used in late texts, e.g. אֲבָל אֲרוֹן הָאֱלֹהִים הֶעֱלָה דָוִיד
מִקִּרְיַת יְעָרִים, 'but David had brought the ark of God up
from Kiriath-jearim' (II Ch 1:4).

555 The conjunction כִּי has adversative force after negatives
(cf. §447), e.g. כִּי־בוֹקֵר אָנֹכִי, 'but I am a herdsman'
(Am 7:14); cf. Gn 17:15. It is commonly reinforced with
pleonastic אִם (cf. §457), e.g. וַיֹּאמְרוּ לֹא כִּי אִם־מֶלֶךְ יִהְיֶה
עָלֵינוּ, 'They said, "No, but there shall be a king over
us"' (I Sm 8:19); cf. Ps 1:2, Dt 7:5.

13 EXCEPTIVE (LIMITATIVE) CLAUSES

556 Marked by כִּי אִם, after a negative or a rhetorical question (cf. §447), e.g. לֹא אֲשַׁלֵּחֲךָ כִּי אִם־בֵּרַכְתָּנִי, 'I will
not let you go, unless you bless me' (Gn 32:27); cf. Am
3:7, Lv 22:6.

557 Introduced by בִּלְתִּי אִם (cf. §422), e.g. הֲיִתֵּן כְּפִיר קוֹלוֹ
מִמְּעֹנָתוֹ בִּלְתִּי אִם־לָכָד, 'Does a young lion growl in its lair
unless it has caught something?' (Am 3:4); also without
pleonastic אִם, e.g. לֹא־תִרְאוּ פָנַי בִּלְתִּי אֲחִיכֶם אִתְּכֶם, 'You
will not see my face unless your brother is with you'
(Gn 43:3); cf. Nu 11:6, Is 10:4.

14 RESTRICTIVE CLAUSES

558 Indicated by means of אֶפֶס כִּי (cf. §427), e.g. אֶפֶס כִּי־עַז
הָעָם הַיֹּשֵׁב בָּאָרֶץ, 'Nevertheless, the people who live in
the land are strong' (Nu 13:28); cf. Ju 4:9, Am 9:8.
When a second כִּי would follow, the first is omitted,
e.g. אֶפֶס כִּי־נִאֵץ נִאַצְתָּ אֶת־אֹיְבֵי י/ בַּדָּבָר הַזֶּה, 'Nevertheless,
because you have shown complete contempt for the enemies

93

(*sic*) of Yahweh in this matter' (II Sm 12:14).

559 By means of the particle אַךְ (cf. §388), e.g. אַךְ הֱיֵה־לִּי לְבֶן־חַיִל, 'However, be valiant for me' (I Sm 18:17); cf. I Kg 17:13, Gn 9:4.

560 By means of the particle רַק (cf. §390), e.g. רַק לָאֲנָשִׁים הָאֵל אַל־תַּעֲשׂוּ דָבָר, 'However, do nothing to these men' (Gn 19:8); cf. Dt 12:15, I Kg 3:3.

15 EQUATIONAL CLAUSES

561 When set in the present, these are non-verbal statements, while in past or future time the verb הָיָה is usually required.

562 With a substantival predicate, e.g. כִּי־אֲנָשִׁים אַחִים אֲנָחְנוּ, 'for we are kinsmen' (Gn 13:8), אֵלֶּה שְׁמוֹת בְּנֵי־עֵשָׂו, 'These are the names of Esau's sons' (Gn 36:10), וַיְהִי־הֶבֶל רֹעֵה צֹאן, 'Abel was a herder of flocks' (Gn 4:2). This frequently occurs when an adjectival predicate might have been expected (cf. §67), e.g. אֱמֶת נָכוֹן הַדָּבָר, 'should the report be true and well founded' (Dt 13:15), אֱמֶת הָיָה הַדָּבָר אֲשֶׁר שָׁמָעְתִּי, 'The report which I heard was true' (I Kg 10:6), הֲשָׁלוֹם בֹּאֶךָ, 'Is your coming peaceable?' (I Kg 2:13). The negative is expressed by means of לֹא (contrast non-existence with אַיִן, §569), e.g. לֹא־אָחִיךָ הוּא, 'He is not your kinsman' (Dt 17:15), לֹא נָבִיא אָנֹכִי, 'I am not a prophet' (Am 7:14) and לֹא־חֹדֶשׁ וְלֹא שַׁבָּת, 'It is neither new moon nor sabbath' (II Kg 4:23, with the subject unexpressed).

563 With an adjectival predicate (cf. §75), e.g. וְעֵינֵי לֵאָה רַכּוֹת, 'Leah's eyes were weak' (Gn 29:17), רָעַתְכֶם רַבָּה, 'Your wickedness is great' (I Sm 12:17), רַבָּה רָעַת הָאָדָם בָּאָרֶץ, 'The wickedness of mankind was great on the earth' (Gn 6:5), וַיְהִי עֵר בְּכוֹר יְהוּדָה רַע בְּעֵינֵי י', 'Judah's first-born Er was wicked in Yahweh's sight' (Gn 38:7); the negative is expressed with לֹא, e.g. לֹא־טוֹב הַדָּבָר, 'The situation is not good' (Ex 18:17).

94

564 With the preposition בְּ of identity (cf. §249) before a substantival predicate, e.g. כִּי־אֱלֹהֵי אָבִי בְּעֶזְרִי, 'for the God of my father was my help' (Ex 18:4); cf. Ps 29:4.

565 With a prepositional phrase as predicate, e.g. הִנֵּה־רִבְקָה לְפָנֶיךָ, 'Here is Rebekah before you' (Gn 24:51), וּדְבַר־ אַבְנֵר הָיָה עִם־זִקְנֵי יִשְׂרָאֵל, 'Abner's communication was with the elders of Israel' (II Sm 3:17); with לֹא in the negative, e.g. לֹא בָרַעַשׁ יי, 'Yahweh was not in the earthquake' (I Kg 19:11); cf. Nu 23:23.

566 With an adverbial predicate, e.g. כִּי זֶבַח הַיָּמִים שָׁם, 'for the annual sacrifice is there' (I Sm 20:6).

16 EXISTENTIAL CLAUSES

567 To express past or future time the verb הָיָה is employed, e.g. אִישׁ הָיָה בְאֶרֶץ־עוּץ, 'There was a man in the land of Uz' (Jb 1:1); with לֹא in the negative, e.g. לֹא־הָיָה שָׁם לֶחֶם כִּי־אִם־לֶחֶם הַפָּנִים, 'There was no bread there except the Presence-bread' (I Sm 21:7).

568 For present time the particle יֵשׁ (cf. §477) may be employed, e.g. אָכֵן יֵשׁ יי בַּמָּקוֹם הַזֶּה, 'Truly Yahweh is in this place' (Gn 28:16); cf. Ru 3:12.

569 Non-existence in the present may be expressed by means of the negative substantive אַיִן (cf. §§407f.), either in the bound form, e.g. בַּיָּמִים הָהֵם אֵין מֶלֶךְ בְּיִשְׂרָאֵל, 'In those days there was no king in Israel' (Ju 21:25), or with the free form in apposition, e.g. וְכֹחַ אַיִן לְלֵדָה, 'There is no strength to give birth' (II Kg 19:3). In two passages the particle יֵשׁ is used redundantly with אַיִן: וְאִין יֵשׁ־פֹּה תַחַת־יָדְךָ חֲנִית אוֹ־חָרֶב, 'Is there no spear or sword here in your possession?' (I Sm 21:9), אַף אֵין־ יֵשׁ־רוּחַ בְּפִיהֶם, 'nor is there breath in their mouths' (Ps 135:17). More rarely the substantive אֶפֶס (cf. §426) may be employed, either in the bound form, e.g. וְאֶפֶס עָצוּר וְאֶפֶס עָזוּב, 'There was neither bond nor free' (II Kg 14:26), or with the free form in apposition, e.g. הָאֶפֶס עוֹד

95

אִישׁ לְבֵית שָׁאוּל, 'Is there no longer any one belonging to Saul's house?' (II Sm 9:3).

17 WORD ORDER

570 With the loss of case endings, word order became an important feature of Hebrew syntax (see p. 3).

Verbal Clauses

571 These are clauses containing verbal forms other than participles or infinitives.

572 The normal order is verbal predicate + noun subject + noun object + adverb or prepositional phrase, e.g. וַיָּבֵא יוֹסֵף אֶת־דִּבָּתָם רָעָה אֶל־אֲבִיהֶם, 'Joseph brought a bad report of them to their father' (Gn 37:2), וַיִּבְרָא אֱלֹהִים אֶת־הָאָדָם בְּצַלְמוֹ, 'God created mankind in his image' (Gn 1:27); cf. Gn 2:8. Expressions of time are usually placed at the beginning, e.g. בָּעֵת הַהִיא אָמַר י׳ אֶל־יְהוֹשֻׁעַ, 'At that time Yahweh said to Joshua' (Jo 5:2), בַּיָּמִים הָהֵם חָלָה חִזְקִיָּהוּ לָמוּת, 'In those days Hezekiah fell mortally ill' (II Kg 20:1). Pronominal objects or prepositions with suffixes may intervene between verb and subject, e.g. וְלֹא־נָשָׂא אֹתָם הָאָרֶץ לָשֶׁבֶת יַחְדָּו, 'The land could not support them living together' (Gn 13:6), וַיֹּאמֶר לָהֶם יוֹסֵף, 'Joseph said to them' (Gn 44:15). Sometimes the position of subject and object is reversed, e.g. וַיַּחְנְכוּ אֶת־בֵּית י׳ הַמֶּלֶךְ וְכָל־בְּנֵי יִשְׂרָאֵל, 'The king and all the Israelites dedicated the house of Yahweh' (I Kg 8:63).

573 The subject may precede the verb: (1) for emphasis, e.g. הַנָּחָשׁ הִשִּׁיאַנִי, 'It was the serpent that deluded me' (Gn 3:13), אֱלֹהִים יִרְאֶה־לּוֹ הַשֶּׂה לְעֹלָה, 'It is God who will see to the sheep for his burnt offering' (Gn 22:8); (2) for contrast, e.g. אַבְרָם יָשַׁב בְּאֶרֶץ־כְּנָעַן וְלוֹט יָשַׁב בְּעָרֵי הַכִּכָּר, 'Abram settled in the land of Canaan, whereas Lot settled among the cities of the Plain' (Gn 13:12), וְחַנָּה לֹא עָלָתָה, 'but Hannah did not go up' (I Sm 1:22); cf. Gn

96

37:11, 4:2; (3) to indicate a change of subject, e.g. וּמַלְכִּי־צֶדֶק מֶלֶךְ שָׁלֵם הוֹצִיא לֶחֶם וָיָיִן, 'Melchizedek king of Salem brought out food and wine' (Gn 14:18), וְרִבְקָה אָמְרָה אֶל־יַעֲקֹב בְּנָהּ, 'Rebekah said to her son Jacob' (Gn 27:6); (4) to express anterior time (equivalent to an English pluperfect; cf. §162, 3), e.g. וְנֹחַ מָצָא חֵן בְּעֵינֵי יי, 'but Noah had found favour in Yahweh's sight' (Gn 6:8); cf. Gn 31:25; (5) to indicate synchronism (cf. §§235, 237), e.g. הוּא־בָא עַד־לֶחִי וּפְלִשְׁתִּים הֵרִיעוּ לִקְרָאתוֹ, 'Just as he was entering Lehi, the Philistines came towards him shouting' (Ju 15:14); (6) when lengthy, the subject may be placed in rhetorical exposure (cf. §35), e.g. הָאִשָּׁה אֲשֶׁר נָתַתָּה עִמָּדִי הִיא נָתְנָה־לִי מִן־הָעֵץ, 'The woman whom you set beside me, she gave me (fruit) from the tree' (Gn 3:12); cf. Ju 13:8; (7) when the subject is an interrogative pronoun, e.g. מִי יַעֲלֶה־לָּנוּ אֶל־הַכְּנַעֲנִי, 'Who will attack the Canaanites for us?' (Ju 1:1).

574 The object may precede the verb: (1) for emphasis, e.g. סֵפֶר הַתּוֹרָה מָצָאתִי בְּבֵית יי, 'The law-book was what I dis-covered in the house of Yahweh' (II Kg 22:8), אֶת־קֹלְךָ שָׁמַעְתִּי בַגָּן, 'It was the sound of you that I heard in the garden' (Gn 3:10); cf. I Sm 8:7; (2) when it is an in-terrogative pronoun, e.g. מֶה־אֶעֱשֶׂה לָאֵלֶּה, 'What shall I do for these?' (Gn 31:43), וְאֶת־מִי עָשַׁקְתִּי אֶת־מִי רַצּוֹתִי, 'Whom have I wronged? Whom have I oppressed?' (I Sm 12: 3); (3) when stressed or cumbersome it may be placed in rhetorical exposure, e.g. וְגַם אֶת־מַעֲכָה אִמּוֹ וַיְסִרֶהָ מִגְּבִירָה, 'And his (grand-)mother Maacah also, he removed her as queen mother' (I Kg 15:13), אֵת־אֲשֶׁר יֹאמַר יי אֵלַי אֹתוֹ אֲדַבֵּר, 'I will speak only what Yahweh says to me' (I Kg 22:14); cf. II Kg 23:19, Gn 13:15.

575 The verb may also be preceded by a prepositional phrase: (1) for emphasis, e.g. בְּזֵעַת אַפֶּיךָ תֹּאכַל לֶחֶם, 'It is by the sweat of your face that you shall eat your food' (Gn 3:19), בַּיַּבָּשָׁה עָבַר יִשְׂרָאֵל אֶת־הַיַּרְדֵּן הַזֶּה, 'It was on dry

97

land that Israel crossed this Jordan' (Jo 4:22); cf.
Gn 2:17; (2) for contrast, e.g. וְאֶל־קַ֫יִן וְאֶל־מִנְחָתוֹ לֹא
שָׁעָ֑ה, 'whereas for Cain and his offering he had no regard' (Gn 4:5); cf. Gn 1:5; (3) when lengthy, it may be
placed in rhetorical exposure, e.g. הַמִּטָּה אֲשֶׁר־עָלִ֫יתָ שָּׁם
לֹא־תֵרֵד מִמֶּ֫נָּה, 'The bed to which you went, you shall not
leave it' (II Kg 1:4).

576 In adverbial clauses (cf. §491) an inverted word order
is usual. The order subject + object or prepositional
phrase + verb may occur, e.g. אִישׁ הַיָּשָׁר בְּעֵינָיו יַעֲשֶׂה, 'in
that everyone did what he considered right' (Ju 17:6),
אִישׁ לְפִי־אָכְלוֹ לָקָ֑טוּ, 'in that each had gathered as much
as he could eat' (Ex 16:18).

Non-Verbal Clauses

577 These fall into two major categories: (1) those which
identify the subject, when the predicate is definite,
and (2) those which classify or define the subject, normally with an indefinite predicate. They are clearly
distinguished by the word order:

578 Identifying clauses, in which both subject and predicate are definite, exhibit the order subject + predicate, e.g. אָנֹכִי אֱלֹהֵי אָבִ֫יךָ, 'I am the God of your father'
(Ex 3:6), זֶה הַדָּבָר אֲשֶׁר תַּעֲשׂוּן, 'This is the thing that you
are to do' (II Kg 11:5). When an anaphoric demonstrative
(cf. §115) is employed, it precedes the predicate, e.g.
יי' הוּא נַחֲלָתוֹ, 'Yahweh is his inheritance' (Dt 18:2).

579 Classifying clauses, in which the predicate is normally
indefinite, have the order predicate + subject, e.g.
נְקִיִּם אֲנַ֫חְנוּ מִשְּׁבֻעָתֵךְ הַזֶּה, 'We shall be free from this oath
of yours' (Jo 2:17), גָּדוֹל עֲוֹנִי מִנְּשֹׂא, 'My punishment is
too great to bear' (Gn 4:13), כִּי־אֲנָשִׁים אַחִים אֲנָ֫חְנוּ, 'for
we are kinsmen' (Gn 13:8), כִּי־כָבֵד הָרָעָב בָּאָ֫רֶץ, 'for the
famine was severe throughout the land' (Gn 12:10), לֹא
אָדָם הוּא, 'He is not a human being' (I Sm 15:29). In אָחִי

98

הוּא, 'He is my brother' (Gn 20:5), the definite predicate is generic, implying 'He is a brother of mine.' A demonstrative functioning as a copula (cf. §115) follows the predicate, e.g. הָאֲנָשִׁים הָאֵלֶּה שְׁלֵמִים הֵם אִתָּנוּ, 'These men are friendly with us' (Gn 34:21).

580 Clauses expressing a wish (cf. §551) have the order predicate + subject when the former is a noun or a participle, e.g. עֵדָה הַמַּצֵּבָה, 'Let the pillar be a witness!' (Gn 31:52), אָרוּר הָאִישׁ אֲשֶׁר־יֹאכַל לֶחֶם הַיּוֹם, 'Cursed be the man who eats food today!' (I Sm 14:28). In poetry this order may be reversed, e.g. אֹרְרֶיךָ אָרוּר, 'May those who curse you be cursed!' (Gn 27:29, Nu 24:9). However, when the predicate is a prepositional phrase, it normally follows, e.g. אֱלֹהִים עִמָּךְ, 'May God be with you!' (Gn 21:22).

581 Interrogative words regularly introduce a clause, e.g. אֵי הֶבֶל אָחִיךָ, 'Where is your brother Abel?' (Gn 4:9), מִי־הָאִישׁ הַלָּזֶה, 'Who is the man yonder?' (Gn 24:65), מַה־שְּׁמוֹ, 'What is his name?' (Ex 3:13).

582 Inversion of word order (i.e. subject + predicate) is characteristic of circumstantial clauses; cf. §494.

18 ELLIPSIS

583 In comparisons:
- Omission of a substantive is regular, e.g. מְשַׁוֶּה רַגְלַי כָּאַיָּלוֹת, 'making my feet like (those of) hinds' (Ps 18: 34 = II Sm 22:34); cf. Ps 92:11.

584 - Omission of a predicative adjective is much less common, e.g. וּפְסִילֵיהֶם מִירוּשָׁלַ͏ִם וּמִשֹּׁמְרוֹן, 'whose images were (greater) than (those of) Jerusalem and Samaria' (Is 10:10), וּמִצָּהֳרַיִם יָקוּם חָלֶד, '<Your> life will rise up (brighter) than noontime' (Jb 11:17); cf. Ps 4:8.

585 Pronouns are frequently omitted when they are clear from the context:

586 - When subject of an infinitive, e.g. בַּהֲפֹךְ אֶת־הֶעָרִים,

99

'when he overthrew the cities' (Gn 19:29), וַיְהִי כִּשְׁמֹעַ
אֶת־הַדָּבָר הַזֶּה, 'now as soon as he heard this message' (I
Kg 20:12).

587 - When subject of a participle, e.g. וְהִנֵּה עֹמֵד, 'while
he was standing' (Gn 24:30), וְגַם הֹלֵךְ לִקְרָאתְךָ, 'as he is
also coming to meet you' (Gn 32:7); cf. Gn 37:15, Am 7:
1, Jo 8:6. Note especially, in an indefinite context,
וְלִבְנִים אֹמְרִים לָנוּ עֲשׂוּ, 'as they say to us, "Make bricks"'
(Ex 5:16).

588 - When object of a verb, e.g. וַיָּבֵא אֶל־הָאָדָם, 'He brought
them to the man' (Gn 2:19), וַתָּשֶׂם אֶל־הַמִּטָּה, 'She put them
in the bed' (I Sm 19:13); cf. I Sm 17:35, Gn 18:7, II
Kg 4:5.

589 Brachylogy, when the common object of a verb is omitted,
e.g. נָשָׂא (קוֹל), 'cry out' (Is 3:7, 42:2), כָּרַת (בְּרִית),
'make a covenant' (I Sm 20:16, II Ch 7:18), שִׂים (לֵב),
'pay attention' (Jb 4:20, Is 41:20), הִפִּיל (גּוֹרָל), 'cast
lots' (I Sm 14:42, Jb 6:27), הֵשִׁיב (דָּבָר), 'respond' (Jb
13:22).

590 After numerals certain expressions, when clear from the
context, are omitted, e.g. שֶׁקֶל (II Sm 18:12, Nu 7:68),
אִישׁ (II Sm 8:13), יוֹם (II Kg 25:1), אֵפָה (Ru 3:15, 17).

591 A verb may be omitted when clear from the context, e.g.
אָבִי יִסַּר אֶתְכֶם בַּשּׁוֹטִים וַאֲנִי בָּעַקְרַבִּים, 'My father chastised
you with whips, but I will chastise you with scorpions'
(II Ch 10:11, 14; contrast I Kg 12:11, 14); cf. Jo 24:
15. This often occurs with the particle פֶּן (cf. §461).

592 Omissions frequently occur with negatives:

593 - אַיִן (cf. §409), e.g. הֲיֵשׁ י' / בְּקִרְבֵּנוּ אִם־אָיִן, 'Is Yahweh
amongst us or not?' (Ex 17:7).

594 - לֹא (cf. §398), e.g. וַיֹּאמֶר לֹא כִּי צָחָקְתְּ, 'He said, "No,
but you did laugh"' (Gn 18:15).

595 - אַל (cf. §403), e.g. אַל בְּנֹתַי, 'No, my daughters' (Ru
1:13), אַל־טַל וְאַל־מָטָר עֲלֵיכֶם, 'Let neither dew nor rain
be upon you' (II Sm 1:21); cf. Is 62:6.

596 The oath formula is sometimes omitted, e.g. אִם־יִרְאֶה אִישׁ בָּאֲנָשִׁים הָאֵלֶּה . . . אֵת הָאָרֶץ הַטּוֹבָה, 'Not one of these men shall see . . . the fine land' (Dt 1:35); cf. Gn 31:52, Jb 1:11.

597 Aposiopesis, i.e. when the conclusion of a statement, such as the apodosis of a conditional sentence, is left out, e.g. אִם־תִּשָּׂא חַטָּאתָם וְאִם־אַיִן מְחֵנִי נָא מִסִּפְרְךָ, 'If you will forgive their sin, (do so)! But if not, just blot me out of your book' (Ex 32:32); cf. I Sm 12:14, Gn 50: 15, Nu 5:20, II Ch 2:2.

598 Occasionally a single word may constitute an elliptical utterance, e.g. וַיֹּאמֶר עֵד, 'They (Heb. he) said, "He is a witness"' (I Sm 12:5), וַתֹּאמֶר שָׁלוֹם, 'She said, "All is well"' (II Kg 4:23, 26), לַשָּׁלָל, 'To the plunder!' (II Kg 3:23).

Selected Bibliography

Andersen, F. I. *The Hebrew Verbless Clause in the Pentateuch* [*Journal of Biblical Literature*, Monograph Series, 14]. Nashville/New York, 1970.
— *The Sentence in Biblical Hebrew* [*Janua linguarum*, Series practica, 231]. The Hague, 1974.
Brockelmann, C. *Hebräische Syntax*. Neukirchen, 1956.
Claassen, W. T. 'The Declarative-Estimative Hiph'il,' *Journal of Northwest Semitic Languages*, 2 (1972), 5-16.
Davidson, A. B. *Hebrew Syntax*. 3rd ed. Edinburgh, 1901.
Donner, H. and Röllig, W. *Kanaanäische und aramäische Inschriften*. 3 vols. Wiesbaden, 1962-4.
Driver, G. R. 'Gender in Hebrew Numerals,' *Journal of Jewish Studies*, 1 (1948), 90-104.
Driver, S. R. *A Treatise on the Use of the Tenses in Hebrew*. 3rd ed. Oxford, 1892.
Goetze, A. 'The So-Called Intensive of the Semitic Languages,' *Journal of the American Oriental Society*, 62 (1942), 1-8.
Gordis, R. 'The Asseverative Kaph in Ugaritic and Hebrew,' *Journal of the American Oriental Society*, 63 (1943), 176-8.
Gordon, C. H. *Ugaritic Textbook* [*Analecta Orientalia*, 38]. Rome 1965.
Hillers, D. R. 'Delocutive Verbs in Biblical Hebrew,' *Journal of Biblical Literature*, 86 (1967), 320-4.
Hoftijzer, J. 'Remarks concerning the Use of the Particle 't in Classical Hebrew,' *Oudtestamentische Studiën*, 14. Leyden, 1965. Pp. 1-99.
Joüon, P. *Grammaire de l'hébreu biblique*. 2nd ed. Rome, 1965. Pp. 289-536.
Kautzsch, E. *Gesenius' Hebrew Grammar*. 26th ed. Oxford, 1898. Pp. 320-533.
Kustár, P. *Aspekt im Hebräischen* [*Theologische Dissertationen*, 9]. Basel, 1972.
Labuschagne, C. J. et al. *Syntax and Meaning: Studies in Hebrew Syntax and Biblical Exegesis* [*Oudtestamentische Studiën*, 18]. Leyden, 1973.
Meek, T. J. 'Again the Accusative of Time in Amos 1:1,' *Journal of the American Oriental Society*, 61 (1941), 190-1.
— 'The Co-ordinate Adverbial Clause in Hebrew,' *American Journal of Semitic Languages*, 47 (1930/1), 51-2.
— 'The Hebrew Accusative of Time and Place,' *Journal of the American Oriental Society*, 60 (1940), 224-33.
— 'Result and Purpose Clauses in Hebrew,' *Jewish Quarterly Review*, 46 (1955/6), 40-3.

— 'The Syntax of the Sentence in Hebrew,' *Journal of Biblical Literature*, 64 (1945), 1-13.

Meyer, R. 'Aspekt und Tempus im althebräischen Verbalsystem,' *Orientalistische Literaturzeitung*, 59 (1964), 117-26.

Nötscher, F. 'Zum emphatischen Lamed,' *Vetus Testamentum*, 3 (1953), 372-80.

Pope, M. H. '"Pleonastic" Wāw before Nouns in Ugaritic and Hebrew,' *Journal of the American Oriental Society*, 73 (1953), 95-8.

Rabin, C. תחביר לשון המקרא. Jerusalem, 1967.

Rubinstein, A. 'A Finite Verb continued by an Infinitive Absolute in Biblical Hebrew,' *Vetus Testamentum*, 2 (1952), 362-7.

Rundgren, F. *Das althebräische Verbum: Abriss der Aspektlehre*. Uppsala, 1961.

Schlesinger, K. 'Zur Wortfolge im hebräischen Verbalsatz,' *Vetus Testamentum*, 3 (1953), 381-90.

Scott, R. B. Y. 'Secondary Meanings of אַחַר, After, Behind,' *Journal of Theological Studies*, 50 (1949), 178-9.

Speiser, E. A. 'Pitfalls of Polarity,' *Language*, 14 (1938), 187-202.

Thomas, D. W. 'A Consideration of Some Unusual Ways of Expressing the Superlative in Hebrew,' *Vetus Testamentum*, 3 (1953), 209-24.

Weingreen, J. 'The Construct-Genitive Relation in Hebrew Syntax,' *Vetus Testamentum*, 4 (1954), 50-9.

Wernberg-Møller, P. 'Observations on the Hebrew Participle,' *Zeitschrift für die alttestamentliche Wissenschaft*, 71 (1959/60), 54-67.

— '"Pleonastic" Waw in Classical Hebrew,' *Journal of Semitic Studies*, 3 (1958), 321-6.

Wevers, J. W. 'Semitic Bound Structures,' *Canadian Journal of Linguistics*, 7 (1961), 9-14.

Index of Cited Passages

Note: All references are to sections only

Genesis

22:12	451
22:13	352
22:14	492
22:16	363, 534
22:18	534
24:4	70, 179
24:6	461
24:8	74, 390
24:12	70, 331
24:18	224
24:19	378, 457, 496
24:22	500
24:25	330
24:30	587
24:35	269
24:42	479
24:51	565
24:54	328
24:56	495
24:58	171, 541
24:65	86, 581
25:1	224
25:6	499
25:11	329
26:8	497
26:11	218
26:24	56
26:27	495
26:28	335
26:29	331, 332, 391
26:33	273, 311
27:3	54
27:4	175, 187, 518, 522
27:6	573
27:10	522
27:15	73, 340
27:21	118
27:29	104, 580
27:33	380, 509
27:34	107, 378
27:36	118
27:42	59, 475
27:45	508
27:46	515
28:5	29
28:9	292
28:15	457
28:16	568
28:17	127
28:20	515
29:7	194
29:17	563
29:19	317
29:27	59
30:8	335
30:16	74
30:31	225
30:34	460, 548
30:36	40, 73
31:8	453
31:13	82
31:14	230
31:15	206, 280
31:20	291, 418, 489

Genesis

31:21	88
31:25	573
31:27	226
31:32	162, 330
31:38	118
31:43	574
31:52	551, 580, 596
32:7	587
32:9	94
32:10	331
32:12	461
32:19	440
32:23	74
32:27	556
32;29	447
32:31	299
34:7	172
34:12	256
34:13	468
34:21	579
34:30	48
35:5	81
36:7	76, 318
36:10	114, 562
37:2	572
37:11	573
37:15	167, 587
37:16	213
37:17	358
37:21	57
37:22	367, 520
37:26	124
37:29	407
37:32	544
38:7	563
38:24	316
39:5	228
39:6	46
39:7	299
39:9	247, 534
39:10	15, 258, 532
39:20	489
39:23	247, 407, 534
40:3	489
40:5	131
40:14	347
40:16	384
41:1	68
41:8	23
41:19	273
41:27	234
41:32	289
41:35	350
41:38	256
41:40	57, 390
41:43	210
41:46	504
41:49	311
42:16	449
42:18	190
42:25	9
42:28	118
42:35	9
42:37	170
43:3	422, 557

Genesis

43:4	479
43:7	167
43:10	118, 166, 449, 516
43:16	62
43:17	62
43:25	167
43:27	67
43:32	168
44:3f.	235
44:4	55
44:7	256
44:15	256, 572
44:16	126, 378
44:20	478
44:22	512
44:28	205, 389
45:4	463
45:28	509
46:4	379
47:6	115
47:18	56, 98
48:7	288
48:19	553
49:7	180
49:25	285, 348
50:15	597
50:19	541

Exodus

1:12	264
2:6	71
2:18	226
2:23	74, 319
3:1	359
3:5	463, 538
3:6	578
3:7	376
3:12	452
3:13	513, 581
4:1	167
4:9	379
4:10	399
5:3	243
5:10	407
5:16	587
5:19	195
6:1	167
6:3	249
7:15	278
7:19	42
7:20	244
9:16	522, 553
9:18	82
9:25	313, 327
9:27	33
10:9	248
10:17	390
12:3	131
12:8	293
12:11	494
12:16	280
12:19	250
12:37	257
12:48	209
12:51	290
13:2	250

107

113

Index of Subjects

Compiled by Fred Guttman, Douglas Hawthorne, Douglas Knight, Bruce Naidoff and Noel Osborn. All references are to sections.

119

120

Index of Hebrew Words